Transportation and Economic Development in Latin America

PRAEGER SPECIAL STUDIES IN
INTERNATIONAL ECONOMICS AND DEVELOPMENT

Transportation and Economic Development in Latin America

Charles J. Stokes

FREDERICK A. PRAEGER, Publishers
New York · Washington · London

The purpose of the Praeger Special Studies is to make specialized research monographs in U.S. and international economics and politics
available to the academic, business, and government communities. For
further information, write to the Special Projects Division, Frederick
A. Praeger, Publishers, 111 Fourth Avenue, New York, N.Y. 10003.

FREDERICK A. PRAEGER, PUBLISHERS
111 Fourth Avenue, New York, N.Y. 10003, U.S.A.
77-79 Charlotte Street, London W.1, England

Published in the United States of America in 1968
by Frederick A. Praeger, Inc., Publishers

© 1968 by Frederick A. Praeger, Inc.

Library of Congress Catalog Card Number: 68-18930

Printed in the United States of America

PREFACE AND
ACKNOWLEDGMENT

Two friends now on the staff of the Brookings Institution have
so greatly influenced my thinking about transport planning and
economic development that I cannot forego the privilege of
acknowledging their contributions. Wilfred Owen paused frequently in his own research on these matters to chat at length
with me and to share his impressions, his experiences, and
his sage and witty comments. Without his impetus, the case
studies contained in this book would never have begun. Joseph
Grunwald has spent so much of his academic life in Latin A-
merica that I, who first came to know him in Chile in 1960,
tend to regard him more as a Latin economist than an American
one. It was his concern with the problems and place of economic development in Latin America that led him to urge me on
many occasions to write. Yet neither of these friends can be
held responsible for the results presented here. They have
been kind, perhaps too kind, in their criticisms, for this book
presents ideas often at variance with theirs.

Beginning in 1944 when I was assigned to Puerto Rico by the
Army, I have developed over the years a deep and abiding interest in Latin American economic development problems. My
Master's thesis dealt, for example, with land tenure reform in
Puerto Rico. Then during the years starting in 1958 when I
served as a Fulbright professor in a succession of Latin American universities, from Ecuador to Argentina and thence to Peru,
including along the way many shorter assignments in most of
the other countries, I came to have a direct role in development
planning if only because my students and colleagues drew me
into their endeavors in the government bureaus where they worked.
To acknowledge by name the many many associates in Latin A-
merica who "educated" me would be impossible, but certainly
Dr. Samuel Gorban, Dean of the Faculty of Economic Sciences
of the National University of Litoral during my tenure there, and
one of the moving forces behind the Association of Latin American Faculties of Economic Sciences, must be mentioned. He,
along with Dr. Carlos Capuñay Mimbela, dean of the Faculty
of Economic Science at San Marcos in Lima, drew me into the
mainstream of economic thinking in Latin America and put me
to work on problems of direct moment to their countries. If
either had had his way, I would not have left Latin America.

Each of the case studies has appeared previously. The Tej-erias-Valencia Autopista study appeared in Spanish in the Revista de Economia Latinoamericana, August, 1965, published by the Central Bank of Venezuela. Its editor, Dr. Luis Pastori has kindly given permission for its inclusion in an English version in this book. By the same token, the editors of the Traffic Quarterly, April, 1966, have given permission for the use of my Carretera Marginal de la Selva article here. Similarly, Dr. Raymond Murphy, editor of Economic Geography, has granted me permission to use "The Freight Transport System of Colombia," January, 1967, as a chapter in this work.

My colleagues in research, Clell Harrel, Lorand Dabasi-Schweng, Eric Dodge, Robert Brown, Edwin Haefele, Gary Fromm, Barbara Berman (now Bergmann), Tillo Kuhn, Leon Hirsch, Martin Klein, Hans Platenius, among many others, were always ready to stop and share their observations. Without the benefit of many conversations with them, my ideas would have lacked some of their sharpness and applicability. Their helpfulness in aiding me to find ways of expressing particular concepts cannot be forgotten.

To acknowledge the contributions of my wife and family in this research is not routine. Anne accompanied me wherever I went in Latin America, setting up home under all sorts of climatic conditions. Kevin went along taking notes and making observations that I have incorporated often without telling him so. And Keith with his knack for making friends gave me frequent opportunity to understand important aspects of the culture the transport investments were designed to change.

The University of Bridgeport was generous in giving me leaves of absence when I needed them and in providing research grants and secretarial assistance. My secretaries, Mrs. Judith Toth and Mrs. Elaine Fraser, along with my research assistant, Mrs. Virginia Iles, aided mightily in the final stages of composition, and their ideas have greatly influenced the editorial form of this work.

Charles J. Stokes

CONTENTS

LIST OF TABLES

LIST OF MAPS

LIST OF CHARTS

Transportation and Economic Development in Latin America

CHAPTER 1 INTRODUCTION

INTRODUCTION

The essence of this book is to be found in the unfolding conclusions to be drawn from the three case studies contained
in Chapters 2, 3, and 4. Each case study examines in some
detail a major transport investment which was designed
to aid in furthering the economic development of a Latin
American nation. The projects studied, a superhighway in
Venezuela, the freight transport system of Colombia and
the dramatic proposals for a Carretera Marginal de la
Selva along the eastern edge of the Andes, possess considerable intrinsic interest both for the layman and for the student
of the relation between transport investment and economic
development. However, in undertaking to combine in one
book an analysis of the economic impact of such widely di-
verse and distant projects, I had some purposes beyond
simply that of case study presentation. These purposes,
to be specific, are to derive some understanding of possible
principles of transport investment in developing countries, to
outline the problems of measuring economic impact of any sort,
to suggest the nature of the evaluation problem both before and
after massive transport investments are made, and to give
some background for a study of economic planning as it relates
to key infrastructure investments. Thus following those chapters
in which the case studies are presented comes one in which we
look at general considerations about such matters, largely based
upon the country case studies.

The justification for seeking new answers in this field of transport investment is easily given. For one thing, there has been
for too long an almost complete separation of engineering decision-
making from the economics of transport. To be sure, an
engineering economics has come into existence, but this branch
of economics, though it was technically well advanced, has not
concerned itself with problems of economic development as such.
The anomaly that a major highway decision, for example, might
be made on engineering capability and intrinsic evaluation, without regard to the role of this investment in achieving what might
be the normal economic development goals of a nation was becoming painfully evident to many observers by the early 1960's.
The practice of insisting upon some form of benefit/cost analysis for each major transport project which had come into vogue
in the post World War II years did not provide as much improvement in the decision-making process as was to be hoped. Partly

3

this was so because there was a tendency for the firms called
upon to make such evaluations always to find in favor of the
proposed project.   It is perhaps unfair to point out that many
of these firms had a financial interest in seeing the projects
undertaken.   It should be added that there was and indeed is
not yet any general agreement about how to use benefit-cost
analysis particularly in an economic environment as uncertain
as that in many developing nations.   It was in this context of
uncertainty and general dissatisfaction that these case studies
were begun.   Their purpose was to look beyond the projects or
transport systems themselves and see what might have happened
or what had appeared to happen to the process of economic
development as these modes of transport were put into use.   An
attempt was made to develop from each case study an understanding of economic impact which might have general
application.

In recent years, considerable advance has been made in the
theory of investment.   Though largely classified under the
heading of capital budgeting, these advances enable us to understand first what a capital investment is: a flow of cash or other
returns over time presumably discounted to the present and regarded as one of a series of possible uses for available funds.
The proper criteria to be used in making a selection among possible investments have been widely and even hotly discussed,
but the applicable principles are generally agreed upon.   Techniques for the costing of available funds have been worked out
as well; and though there is less agreement here, yet the principles are sufficiently understood so that most scholars go about
the matter in similar ways.   The question, however, is: How
relevant are such advances to the selection among competing
transport investment and indeed all forms of investment in developing countries ?   It is significant that less use has been made
than might have been expected of these techniques in the many
engineering studies used as bases for decision by international
lending agencies, national planning boards, and such foreign aid
entities as the Agency for International Development of the United
States.

One of the reasons for this lack of use may be that the planning
context for the transport decision tends to emphasize different
variables than those used in the decision models presented in
ordinary capital budgeting.   Theories of planning are even more
recent in being worked out than those of capital budgeting and

relatively little integration between such theories has been
essayed as yet. A suggestion along these lines, however, is
contained in an appendix to Chapter 5. Each transport investment is so massive with respect to the economy into which
it is being placed that questions about alternative uses of the
available funds, about the cost of these funds and the like,
seemed of less importance than the "look" of the economy with
the investment in place. What were the effects, the changes,
the energies released, the economic resources displaced, the
economic activities encouraged and discouraged, the administrative techniques made possible, the political integration
achieved, and thus the national economic development accom-
plished by the investment? Economists were understandably
reluctant to let such decisions hang on the slender evidence
presented by capital budgeting tools.

Yet it was counsel of despair indeed to argue that there was
nothing that economists could say about improving the choice
mechanism available to political administrators in respect of
transport investment. This would have tended to remand the
issue to the level of bureaucratic know-how where the government department best staffed with engineering talent was likely
to be the source of the project proposals most likely to be
accepted. In many Latin American countries, this department
is the Ministry of Public Works with well-trained highway personnel. In India, by contrast, it would be the railway administration. In any case, the investment most likely to be made
would be that project which could be prepared quickest, de-
fended most readily before financing agencies, and put in place
for development and political impact as soon as possible. Just
as Mount Everest was climbed because it was there, so in the
absence of competent economic advice transport decisions will
tend to take priority over other development decisions because
the staff is there ready to work.

Latin America was chosen for these case studies largely because in few other areas of the world is transport so crucial to
economic development. The barriers imposed by mountains,
jungle, desert, rivers, and oceans are impressive enough; but
at this stage of continental development with settlement limited
largely to peripheral areas along the coastlines, any major advance in living standards seems to depend upon ways to integrate small national economies at least in some basic economic
fashion. Efforts toward the creation of a common market are

in this direction and would require for their fruition far better
transport connections than now exist.   To be sure, Latin America is also considerably ahead of most parts of Asia and Africa
and frequently on a level with nations in Eastern Europe.   That
is to say, in terms of economic development, Latin America is
a kind of middle kingdom.   This raises the question of the applicability of conclusions drawn from Latin America to other parts
of the developing third world.   Though there will be little counter-
part in all but the most advanced nations to some of the problems
presented by the autopista from Tejerias to Valencia in Venezuela,
certainly few parts of the world have development at levels as
low as those to be encountered along the route of the Carretera
Marginal de la Selva.   Moreover the problems of freight transport in Colombia run the gamut of transport modes and investment decisions likely to be faced anywhere.   In no case are the
problems of Latin American transport and economic development
more nearly like those of the United States than those of Africa
or Asia.

The case studies presented here began as illustrative efforts
for the Transport Research Project at the Brookings Institution
during my tenure of membership on the senior staff of that organization, 1963-64.   I continued to work on them while I served
as catedratico in economic development and planning at the Major
University of San Marcos in Lima, the academic year 1964.   It
was while I was in Lima that I began to be urged to collect my
studies and to prepare a book which would be of use to transport
and development planners everywhere.   But the defense for
another book is not simply that there is a lack of adequate trea-
tises on a particular subject, but rather that the author has a
contribution to make derived from his studies and his mature
judgment.   The delay until now was then caused by the doubt
that as yet I had anything significant to say.   Now that I have put
my thoughts on paper, my readers will have to determine the
value of my findings and evaluations.

What follows, then, is an essay on economic development, first,
and then on choice among transport modes as development investments.   It will have served a useful purpose if it turns out
to be relevant to current discussion on development policy in the
United States and Latin America.   It is my feeling that the emerging generations of economists and political leaders in Latin America as I have come to know them over many years are anxious to

know how to transform their nations as rapidly as possible. This book is designed to help them "a fin de que no tropiecen en sus esfuerzos."

CHAPTER 2   **2**   TEJERIAS-
VALENCIA
AUTOPISTA
IN
VENEZUELA

TEJERIAS-VALENCIA AUTOPISTA IN VENEZUELA

In 1958,[1] Venezuela completed its second major autopista, a
limited access highway from Tejerias to Valencia. This highway which parallels the Pan American Highway as well as the
Central Railway of Venezuela is one of the largest such projects
in Latin America Was it necessary to make such a massive investment in highways? What has been the effect of this investment upon the Aragua Valley through which it passes? Upon the
city of Caracas? Upon the national economy of Venezuela?

In this chapter, because we recognize the frequently made criticisms of Venezuelan public works that they are unnecessarily
expensive and are built more for the impression they make than
for the service they render, we begin by analyzing the decision
to build the Tejerias-Valencia autopista. In this analysis, we
attempt to see what criteria of need existed and how they were
used. We also examine the possibility of improvements to the
existing Pan American Highway. And we finish the analysis by
considering a major improvement in the railway as an alternative.
We find that the decision was in many ways justifiable.

Next we examine the impact of the highway upon the valley itself. We do this within the context of a theoretical analysis of
the development process in Venezuela. This enables us to see
changes in the relative economic importance of Aragua and Carabobo states within the nation. It also permits us to see what
changes take place in the economic structure of Venezuela which
can be traced to the highway. And lastly we see how the urban
landscape of the Aragua Valley has been affected by the presence
of the new highway.

Having seen what the decision was, why it was made and what
the results of that decision were, we then attempt an evaluation
of the benefits obtained from this investment. In the first instance, we consider only those benefits which accrue to the users
of the highway, either the shippers or the truckers and motorists.
We compare these user or shipper benefits with the cost involved
in the construction and maintenance of the highway and thus obtain various measures of the net benefit. Because direct net
benefits are obtained, less emphasis is laid upon what have
been called the development benefits; but these are outlined next
with an attempt to spell out those which are the results of the
highway in contrast with any other possible transport investment.

The conclusion we reach is that at least in this case the criticisms of highway construction in Venezuela have missed the mark. We show conclusively that a massive highway investment was necessary and that it had substantial direct and developmental benefits. We also demonstrate that as a consequence of such massive investments the social cost of transport in Venezuela is not only much lower than in most underdeveloped nations but also lower than in many advanced nations.

ANALYSIS OF THE DECISION TO BUILD
TEJERIAS-VALENCIA AUTOPISTA

In this portion of this chapter, we seek not so much to determine how the decision to build an autopista was arrived at, but rather what alternative could have or did face the Venezuelan Ministry of Public Works (MOP) at the time the decision was made   We attempt to analyze the elements that a rational highway decision process ought to have taken into account, limiting ourselves in this instance to the direct cost of the project and of its alternatives.

We do this first because it was in this context that the decision was actually made and in terms of which the MOP currently evaluates the effects of its decision. To be sure, we may now possess information which the MOP did not have, but in setting out the extreme positions on an "as if" basis, we are better able fairly to judge the decision in its own terms. In later parts, we work out other criteria which may be applied to an evaluation of this decision.

First, we examine the need criteria used by the MOP. In the second section, we consider the alternative of major improvements to the existing two-lane Pan American Highway. And then we take improvements in the existing railway as an alternative to either of the possible highway decisions. Finally, we present the actual decision with its resultant direct costs.

Measures of Need

The basic criterion for highway investment in Venezuela during the postwar period is need as indicated by the capacity of existing facilities. Here we spell out the various measures of capacity and apply these measures to the highway and the railway.

Before the building of the autopista, the route between Valencia and the gateway to the Caracas Valley at Tejerias was served by a single-track narrow-gauge railway and by a two-lane highway. The railway--the Central Railway of Venezuela--had probably reached capacity use in 1944 when some 23,000,000 ton kilometers of freight and some 507,000 passengers were moved between Caracas and Valencia. The effect of the war upon motor vehicle imports forced shippers to use this route to an extent never before reached so that though precise estimates of capacity are not available, this all-time high level of use must be regarded as in some sense a practical capacity.

The Pan American Highway was relatively modern in the early 1950's. It was a two-lane paved road with a width of 10.3 meters in rural stretches. The pavement was 2 centimeters of bituminous macadam with a 30 centimeters stone and gravel foundation. Still very much in existence, it leads through each of the valley towns and in the urban stretches is substantially narrower than in the rural portions.

An origin and destination survey made in 1959 revealed that some 285 million ton kilometers of freight were moving by highway through the Aragua Valley along with some 10 million ton kilometers by rail. [2]

Clearly this total traffic was above the capacity of the railway without major improvements such as double tracking and the removal of tortuous curves in the mountainous sections between Tejerias and Caracas. And if the railway was incapable of handling any significant share of the actual freight movement in the late 1950's the highway was also carrying traffic well above its rated capacity. For all type C roads in Venezuela, the classification assigned by the MOP to the Pan American Highway, the World Bank has estimated capacity to be between 200 and 600 vehicles per day. [3] Somewhat more realistically, Richard Soberman working out practical capacities for similar highways in the Guayana uses estimates ranging from 2,000 to 3,500 vehicles per day. And even if we correct his estimates for street widths in the colonial towns through the Pan American passes, [4] we are still left with between 1,500 and 2,000 vehicles per day.

But these comments lead naturally to the question of how best to determine the capacity of a highway. The World Bank's estimates are based upon an examination of the basic design standards. Soberman takes into account the physical features of the highway itself, its terrain, and the composition of the vehicle fleet along with traffic flows characteristic of Venezuelan highways. Another approach due to Meiberg[5] would regard the range of existing traffic flows on type C highways, for example, as the possible supply of transport services. For the construction of a demand curve, we would rely upon estimates of vehicle-operating costs. Thus in Chart 1 we trace as a demand curve the relation between average vehicle-operating costs (in centimos of bolivares) for each type of highway in Venezuela and the actual average vehicle count per day (for the years 1960-61).

For each type of highway, the supply curve is drawn up on the assumption that at the average vehicle count per day, congestion costs (which are in effect marginal vehicle-operating costs) are zero and that at the maximum recorded count by this type of highway those costs are equal to the cost of shifting from a better to a lower design highway. Thus S_2 is the supply curve for type D highways.

The intersection of the supply and demand curves yields then an effective capacity estimate. This figure for type C highways in Venezuela is about 3,800 vehicles per day. That is to say, given the design characteristics of highways, the costs of vehicle operating and actual traffic movement, 3,800 vehicles per day is an amount which can be carried by this type of highway without resort to major highway improvements in order to lower costs which would permit substantial increments in traffic.

As Meiberg points out, the implication of this analysis is that congestion itself may be one of the efficient ways to "expand" highway services. But whichever one of these estimates we choose, the Pan American Highway was well in excess of its capacity. On such sections as Turmero-Maracay, traffic had reached 1,300 vehicles per day by 1941. This same section by 1954 was carrying traffic in excess of 4,500. Maximums in the vicinity of 7,000 vehicles per day were being recorded in the Tejerias-La Victoria sector by the middle 1950's.[6] Thus transport costs could have been reduced by an increase in the transport capacity of the route.

CHART 1

DETERMINATION of EFFECTIVE
CAPACITY of FIVE TYPES of
HIGHWAYS
VENEZUELA 1962

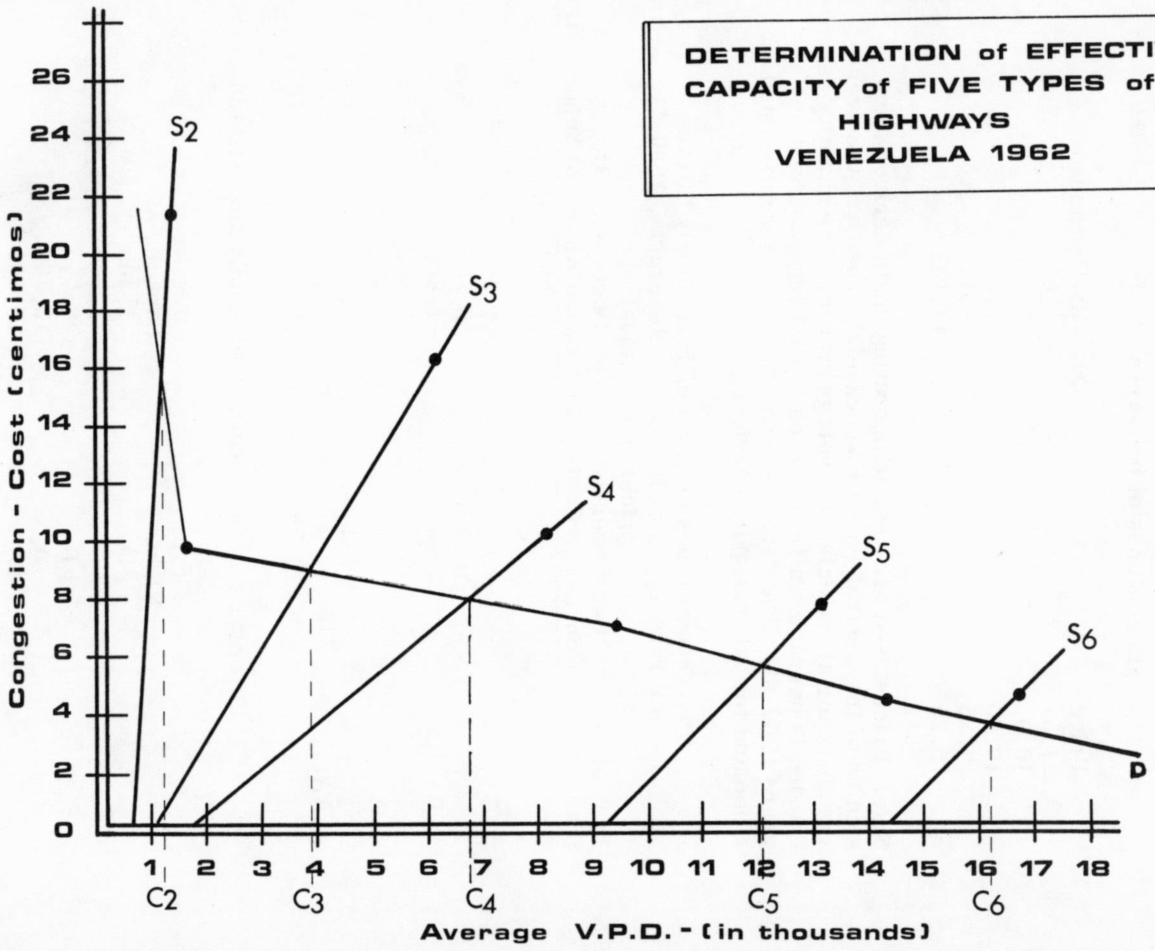

Five Observations on a Demand Curve for Highway services, Venezuela, 1960-61 (prices
in centimos of bolivares)

Price	Quantity Demanded
21.5	650
16.0	1,300
10.00	1,844
7.25	9,171
5.25	14,133

Note: Prices used are vehicle operating costs derived from
studies of the Central Bank of Venezuela. They are the average costs for all vehicles at average traffic. The quantity de-
manded is average traffic for each type of highway for the
years 1960-61. The data are treated as if they represented
a demand for all transport services.

Two Observations on Each of Five Supply Curves
for Five Types of Highways, Venezuela, 1960-61
(prices in centimos)

Type of Highway	Two Observed Congestion Costs	Two Observed Utilization Amts.	Designation of Supply Curve
D	0	650	
	21.5	1,300	S_2
C	0	1,300	
	16.0	5,800	S_3
B	0	1,844	
	10.0	8,250	S_4
A	0	9,171	
	7.25	13,000	S_5
AA	0	14,133	
	5.25	16,550	S_6

Capacities as Intersections of Supply and Demand Curves

Type Highway	Effective Capacity
D	1,300
C	3,800
B	6,900
A	12,200
AA	16,100

Improving the Pan American Highway

An alternative facing the Ministry of Public Works was that of improving the Pan American Highway. This could have meant widening the rural stretches and the building of urban bypasses for major towns along the route. Soberman worked out for 1962 possible costs of highways in Venezuela based upon estimated ranges of traffic. If we use these figures--as they appear in Chart 2--the costs of improving the Pan American Highway would be about Bs 50,000 for each additional 2,000 vehicles or so. These costs refer to widening the lanes and the shoulders and not to grade reduction, increases in sight distances, and reduction in horizontal curvature. If we add in maintenance which was estimated by the World Bank to be about Bs 6,000 per kilometer, it is apparent that it would have taken Bs 173,000 per kilometer to provide a highway just adequate to take care of traffic in 1959. For the route between Tejerias and Valencia, this comes to about Bs 21 million to keep vehicle operating costs no higher than they were in the early 1950's.

This estimate involves no land damages and does not take into account the probable cost of three urban bypasses (Turmero, Maracay, and Valencia)--Bs 19 million or 30 kms of bypass at Bs 625,000 per kilometer. A total of Bs 40 million, then, would have permitted the construction of a highway which would have met the need in 1959. This conservative estimate is chosen because to go beyond it would involve such substantial changes that the proposed improvement becomes, in fact, equivalent to the autopista which was built.

In short, the traffic need was greater than a piecemeal solution could be expected to handle. It would, of course, have been possible to allow congestion to act as a rationer of transport services or in some sophisticated way to devise highway user charges which would permit the flow of traffic thought to be most beneficial to the valley's and the nation's economy. It should be noted, however, that forecasted truck traffic alone would have been in excess of effective capacity by the middle 1960's.

Improving the Railway as an Alternative

Venezuelans have frequently argued that a national railway network was necessary either as an alternative or as a supplement

to the highway system.   Faced with the need for further major
highway expenditures in Central Venezuela, a Railway Economic
Commission was set up to examine the feasibility of rail investments.   Using the information and the arguments contained in
the Commission's report, it is possible to work out the cost of
improving the railway between Caracas and Valencia and thus
to make a comparison of a first-class rail service against an
autopista. [7]

Of course, the Central Railway of Venezuela could not have been
used in its present condition.   It is interesting, however, to note
that freight traffic on this railway after having reached a low in
1955 had continued to climb and was by 1962 more than half of
the 1944 level.   Passenger traffic, to be sure, had reached 12%
of the 1944 level.   Apparently building materials and some goods
requiring special handling were moving preferentially by rail.
Though average railway hauls were much longer than truck hauls
(129 kms as against 45) in the Aragua Valley, apparent costs per
ton kilometer on the railway were four to five times higher than
by truck. [8]

The Railway Economic Commission's report set the annual cost
of a railway per kilometer at about the cost of an expressway.
According to its formula and depending upon the rate of interest
used, the breakeven ton-kilometer level which would justify such
a rail investment was about 93 million. [9]

At such a level, freight costs by rail would be equal to the ton-
kilometer costs by truck.   The Railway Commission argued that
beyond this tonnage for trips in excess of 80 kilometers, the
per ton-kilometer cost for rail would level out at about 6 centimos.   Because the commission found truck costs to be in the
vicinity of 12 centimos, they saw a clear advantage in the rail
investment and recommended it.   A Central Bank trucker survey
which put operating costs on this highway in 1959--the year for
which the railroad data are applicable, which is before the completion of the valley portion of the expressway--at between 6
and 7 centimos casts doubt upon any such advantage.

The Railway Commission tended, moreover, to underestimate
the cost of railway construction.   For example, the Commission
found construction costs for the valley to be about Bs 700,000
per kilometer and in the mountain stretch to be about Bs 1,100,000

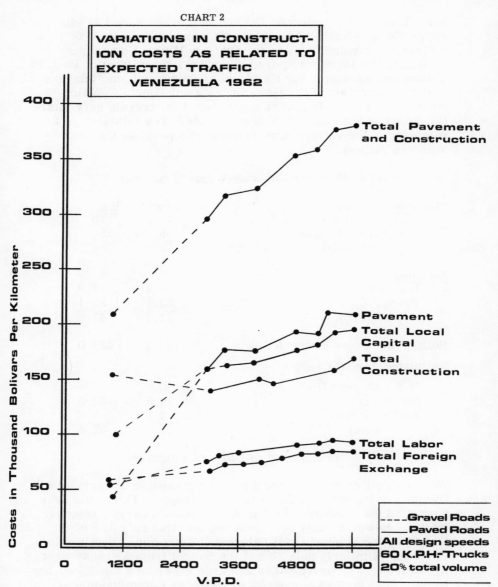

CHART 2

**VARIATIONS IN CONSTRUCT-
ION COSTS AS RELATED TO
EXPECTED TRAFFIC
VENEZUELA 1962**

Costs in Thousand Bolivars Per Kilometer

400

350

300

250

200

150

100

50

0

0   1200   2400   3600   4800   6000

V.P.D.

• Total Pavement
and Construction

• Pavement

Total Local
Capital

Total
Construction

Total Labor

Total Foreign
Exchange

-----Gravel Roads
——Paved Roads
All design speeds
60 K.P.H.-Trucks
20% total volume

Source: Richard M. Soberman, The Cost of Road Transportation
in Venezuela, April 17, 1963. p.34

per kilometer. By contrast the recently constructed 27 kilometer Guanta-Naricual railway cost an average of Bs 2. 6
million per kilometer.   And the Orinoco Mining Company on
relatively flat terrain required an average investment of Bs 1. 25
million per kilometer for its 146 kilometer line in the Guayana.
In the construction of the Gran Ferrocarril Puerto Cabello ,
costs of Bs 1. 7 million were encountered for terrain very similar to that in the Caracas-Valencia route.   The following is a
summary of the estimated investment in a possible Caracas-
Valencia railway.

Cost of Possible Caracas-Valencia Railway

Construction Costs	Low	High
Valley, 100 kms	70	130
Mountains, 40 kms	95	250
Sub Total	165	380
Equipment Costs		
Locomotives	8. 4	17. 9
Freight Cars	23. 1	25. 1
Sub Total	31. 5	43. 0
Rolling Stock plus Construction	196. 3	423. 0
Estimated Annual Charges		
(8% - 30-year life)		
Construction	14. 7	33. 8
Rolling Stock	2. 8	3. 6
Total	17. 5	37. 4

(Figures in millions of Bolivars)

When built, this railway would have been capable of carrying all
freight moving between Caracas and Valencia.   This could have
permitted the highway--the Pan American--to carry passenger
traffic.   However, this overlooks the fact that only 35% of the
freight by ton shipped from Valencia in 1959 was[10] destined for
Caracas.   Similarly only 28% of the freight from Maracay went
to Caracas.   The percentages are even lower on a ton-kilometer
basis.   That is to say, even by the Railway Commission's
reckoning, the advantages of the rail route would apply to a
much smaller than capacity traffic for the rail facility and that

between 60% and 80% of the current traffic would continue to move by highway on a cost advantage basis alone.

Unless this route is part of a national system of rail transport which would generate traffic elsewhere, it does not appear that a first-class rail route was a feasible alternative.

The Autopista--The Ultimate Decision

The actual construction costs of the autopista as completed in 1961--though major sections had been open as early as 1958-- were Bs 355 million. This, of course, was substantially higher than the estimated Bs 146 million when the project was approved. Moreover, maintenance costs have been much higher than anticipated, averaging some Bs 51 thousand per kilometer as against Bs 31,500 expected. The resulting four-lane, wide-shoulder, limited-access tollway cost less than the high estimates for the railway though the highway figures do not, of course, take into account rolling stock. It is likely, however, that trucks and passenger motor vehicles as elements of the national transport investment picture would have increased even in the absence of this particular highway project.

Construction and Maintenance Costs for
Aragua Valley Autopista, Venezuela

	Cost of Construction	Maintenance
Initial Estimate	Bs 146 million	Bs 31,500 per km
Actual Final Cost	Bs 355 million	Bs 51,000 per km

In terms of what a particular budgeted amount in transport investment programs can do in lowering transport costs and increasing capacity along important routes, the decision of the Ministry of Public Works appears to have been a correct one. Nothing other than a very high capacity autopista would have met the need criteria at a low per-vehicle unit cost.

It is, however, not enough to judge a particular project and especially one in a developing nation on need criteria alone. This is even less advisable when the need criteria applied refer only to local situations and do not permit comparison among alternatives elsewhere in the nation. The fact that Venezuela could afford to build a highway costing more than a million dollars a kilometer is a detail which indicates how different Venezuela is

from many other underdeveloped nations, but it does not answer
the question as to whether this more than $100 million could not
have been put to better development effect elsewhere.   To answer
this kind of question, it will be necessary to see the highway in
a larger context.

DIRECT BENEFITS OF THE TEJERIAS-
VALENCIA AUTOPISTA

What can be said about the benefits which accrued directly to
the users of the autopista when once it had been finished? Essentially these benefits involve savings in operating costs and
in time resulting from the availability of a more efficient facility.
To be sure, these benefits also arise from the fact that given the
supply of transport facilities--that is to say, the capacity of the
rail and highway routes in the Aragua Valley--as compared with
the demand, as measured by the excessive traffic densities on
the Pan American Highway, costs were high for all users.   This
fact surely influenced the magnitude of the benefits derived from
the new facility.

Three kinds of savings are considered in this section.   The first
of these is the saving in time, the result of greater speeds on
the new highway.   The time savings are, however, difficult to
translate into money.   What we present here are the shorter
times estimated by the author and the evaluation of these savings
based upon studies by the Corporacion Venezolana de Guayana. [11]

Shipper savings are next and are determined by comparing the
weighted[12] average rate charged by truckers using the route in
the preautopista period with that rate charged in 1962.   Partly,
this comparison is possible because of the impact of the depressed
conditions in 1961--the result of the revolution--which apparently
forced truckers to pass along to shippers the actual reductions in
costs.   Rates fell by about Bs 15 a ton.

Operating costs, the last of the three, also fell.   These are estimated by analysis of reports on truck costs by the Central Bank
of Venezuela and of material provided by the World Bank.   These
estimates permit a comparison of costs on each of the types of

highways in Venezuela.   The technique used here is to assign to the Pan American Highway the operating costs (per vehicle-kilometer) for Type C (or 3) highways and to the autopista those applicable to Type AA (or 6).   This is probably more valid for the autopista than for the Pan American Highway since the Pan American had far higher traffic densities than most Type C highways in the nation.   The savings, of course, are the differences in operating costs between the two types of highways and represent not only an operating-cost saving but in some sense also the cost of relieving congestion.

Which of these savings or what combination of them should we use in estimating the direct savings attributable to this highway?

Calculation of Time Savings

	Distance	Time from End to End	
		Car	Truck
Pan American	123 kms	2 hrs	3 hrs
Autopista	99 kms	1:10	1:50
Saving	24 kms	0:50	1:10

		Car	Truck
Assume value of Bs 4/hr for truck and Bs 3 for car		Bs 2.5 per car	Bs 4.7 per truck
Assume 1962 traffic of 12,013 cars and 2,120 truck per day times 365 days		Bs 11 million	Bs 3.6 million

Total value of time savings per year: Bs 14.6 million

The time savings come to about Bs 15 million a year which would not be enough in themselves to justify the construction of the autopista.   But they surely led to a reduction in both operating costs and freight rates, the latter as a result of the former.

We get the freight-rate saving by inquiring about rates in existence during the 1950's and comparing these with those in effect in 1961.   As observed above, we are helped by the fact of a depression in 1961 which can be presumed to have forced truckers to lower their rates.   And the further fact that Central Bank surveys do not show any drop in truckers' net profits for 1961 helps sustain our analysis. The freight rate or shippers' savings are much more than sufficient to justify the highway costs but represent only a small share of the actual movement along the highway.

Calculation of Shippers' Savings

Caracas-Valencia Route

Rates in	1960	1961	Saving
Organized Truckers	Bs 45	Bs 26	Bs 19
Unorganized Truckers	40	25	15
Average Weighted by Volume	40.4	25.1	15.3

Assume 1959 Freight Movement of 4.99 million tons[13]

Total Shippers' Savings per year: Bs 76.4 millions

The use of operating-cost savings will permit us to account for both freight and passenger movements.   These savings per vehicle-kilometer amount to Bs 0.36, and they account for a

Calculation of Operating Cost Savings

Type of Highway	Cars/Veh/km	Trucks/Veh/km	Wtd. Average
Pan American	Bs 0.25	Bs 1.05	Bs 0.55
Autopista	0.15	0.45	0.19
Saving	0.10	0.60	0.36

saving of Bs 252 million if we compare the total cost of moving the actual traffic in 1962 over the Pan American Highway--which among other things assumes that this would have been possible.

If we use the operating-cost savings in our calculation of the benefit-cost ratio, we obtain   a figure indicating annual return on each bolivar invested, 8.33.

Calculation of Benefit-Cost Ratio

Type of Road	Length	Vehicle Operating Cost	Traffic	Year	Total Operating Cost
Pan American	123 km	Bs 0.55	14,133	365	Bs 349 million
Autopista	99 km	0.19	14,133	365	97 million

Operating Cost Saving (Annual)   Bs 252 million

Cost of New Highway Facility

Annual Cost of Autopista (30 yrs. at 8%)	Bs 29 million
Annual Maintenance Cost	5.1 million
Total Autopista	Bs 34.1 million
Less: Replacement Cost of Pan American	
Annual Construction Costs	Bs 3.2 million
Maintenance Costs	0.8 million
Total Pan American	Bs 4.0 million
Net Additional Cost	Bs 30.1 million

BENEFIT-COST RATIO $\dfrac{252}{30.1} = 8.33$

It must be observed that these traffic counts are very high and approach those in advanced nations. They reflect high per capita income levels as well as stage of development, but they also indicate the extent to which a facility of this magnitude was necessary. Thus, it is that the excess demand for a new highway leads to the high benefit-cost ratio. If the Ministry of Public Works had used the World Bank and similar estimates of capacity of highways, it would have had to be replacing the Aragua Valley through route with new facilities on a frequency which would have involved probably quite prohibitive costs. Another way of putting the matter is to observe that given the usual lead time between the beginning of planning and final construction of a highway, anything less than this facility would have involved the Ministry in constant construction and replacement in this area.

To have obtained a substantial benefit-cost ratio would in normal circumstances have been enough to justify this highway project, but in the present case we want to explore the development effects of this decision. That is to say, now that we know why the Ministry of Public Works felt some action was necessary and why it built this highway as well as knowing the benefit-cost ratio which aids us to evaluate this decision, we want also to know what the decision means for the development of the region served by the highway and the nation at large.

ECONOMIC EFFECTS OF THE HIGHWAY

Now we outline the actual developmental impact of the highway upon the economy of the Aragua Valley and of the Venezuelan nation. That the highway itself is but another chapter in a development story that extends well beyond the decision to build the highway into a series of events that gave rise to the rapid changes going on in Venezuela needs, of course, to be stressed. The highway is thus as much a result of the development along its route as it is a cause. Separating out these elements will be difficult, but we try to put the highway into a context that will help us understand better its impact.

The analysis of the decision to build the highway was also in effect an analysis of the changes in demand for transport services

in the Aragua Valley   Behind this growth in the demand was,
of course, a growth in economic activity in the valley and elsewhere in Venezuela. By the same token, our analysis of the
direct benefits of the highway requires for a complete appreciation of the significance of the magnitudes of benefits, the fact
that the autopista permitted the supplying of transport services at
substantial reductions in cost, however measured. Thus we
have already looked at the direct implications of this change in
the transport demand and supply situation in the Aragua Valley.
What we need next is a more complete explanation of the development process in Venezuela and in the Aragua Valley in order that
we may see why the highway had the effects it did have. In this
way we hope to draw lessons that may have application to our
problem--the general one--of explaining the role of transport
in economic development in Latin America.

Background: Development of the Oil Industry

The timing and spatial characteristics of Venezuelan economic
development in recent decades have been largely affected by the
success of its export sector, the technological nature of the export industry itself, as well as the effects of the distribution of
the income obtained in the export sector. The exploitation of
the oil deposits in the Lake Maracaibo region, as well as to the
East on the llanos beginning essentially in the late 1930's but
having its major impact in the postwar period, permitted Venezuela to create a new economy which did not really replace the
old but was imposed upon it. The significance of this fact is
that the analyst must be careful to avoid assigning to the growth
sector responsibility for the observable sharp contrasts

The development of the petroleum deposits required almost from
the start the making of a transport decision. That decision involved, of course, the provision of pipelines and storage facilities within the country and of adequate shipping facilities to
overseas markets. It is important to observe that this decision
made by the private companies given the task of marketing (and
of course producing) the oil did not have a direct impact upon
the rest of the economy. Pipelines, while they can be made to
carry other commodities besides oil, did not in the Venezuelan
case provide transport facilities that could have been beneficial
to other sectors of the economy. [14]

Because the demand for oil was high, the supply plentiful, and
the spread between cost and price generous, a substantial flow
of foreign exchange was almost immediately available to Venezuela.[15] But while it is useful to trace the inflow of money and
to see how it was distributed, it must be remembered that there
were other almost as important consequences to Venezuela of
the success of this industry. Among these were the technological education given to Venezuelans--a small number, relatively,
to be sure--working in the petroleum industry, the entrepreneurial know-how demonstrated and encouraged and the implications for large numbers of people of evident success in economic
activities quite different from those followed traditionally both in
the petroleum zone and elsewhere in Venezuela. There was
also the provision by the oil companies of a wide range of infrastructure investments--schools, hospitals, water and sewage
systems, housing, stores, and marketing systems, highways
and streets. And to this list must be added the advantage provided by the very large in-migration of skilled workers.[16]

Given the apparently unlimited developable resources at hand
and the excellent overseas market, there was quite naturally a
very rapid development in the oil regions. But the effect of this
bonanza was felt far outside the Lake Maracaibo region and the
boom towns scattered across the Llanos. For this some explanation is needed since, of course, the region along the Valencia-
Tejerias autopista not only is not an oil-producing region but lies
hundreds of kilometers away from such areas.

The Growth of Caracas

It could be argued that it would have been natural to have expected the capital city, Caracas, to have benefited greatly from
the development of industry. But Caracas, after all, not only was
not a port city--as was the case of Buenos Aires, for example--
it was some distance from the growth regions and linked to them
by very inadequate transport systems. Moreover, though Maracaibo
was a tropical city in contrast to the pleasant temperate zone
climate of Caracas, the example of Guayaquil (the Ecuadorian tropical
city) growing at the expense of the temperate zone capital, Quito,
because of its port facilities is at least instructive. It is, however, a
fact that Caracas was the center of economic growth in Venezuela to
an extent far greater than had been the case in the longer previous
period of growth of Guayaquil based upon traditional industries.

The Aragua Valley with its much larger agricultural resources and its equally difficult access to the sea had at various times in the past been a challenger to the Caracas Valley for the location of the national capital. And what evidence is available suggests that prior to the oil boom, the standard of living in that valley was at least as high as that in the Caracas Valley and thus one of the highest in the nation.

Caracas grew, and with its growth came some notable economic advantages. For one thing, the very fact that the growth came to be felt to a major extent in the capital rather than alone in the producing regions led to the avoidance of some of the basic characteristics of a "dual economy." That is to say, the base was laid for a spread of the impact of the oil boom to every corner of the nation. For another, and apparently in contrast to the previous observation, the increase in consumer demand which resulted from the increased purchasing power was in the first instance concentrated geographically. Thus, not only were thresholds for conversion to domestic production passed for increasing numbers of industries as incomes continued their rise, but also income increases were largely concentrated in zones where transport costs internally were low. For these reasons, the initial development impact of higher incomes was largely successful. It is useful to contrast this experience with that of Colombia where because of distance of population centers from the ports, a significant share of the export surplus has had to be devoted to internal transport costs or, analogously, internal transport costs have acted as a kind of tariff protecting domestic industries.

Once embarked on a path of rapid growth, the new industries created by the income rise tended to be located in Caracas. There was in the city the quantity and range of qualities of labor needed for modern industry. There also was the range of ancillary services (including government) and goods which are essential to industrial development. But these had been attracted there by the growth process itself. Growth fed upon growth. And the odd fact is that by the middle fifties, the level of living in Caracas was many times higher than in the producing fields and elsewhere in the nation. Odd because it might have been expected that the oil regions would have retained at least a parity with Caracas, this fact points up the momentum gained by the Caracas economy when once it had been started on its growth path.

A growing Caracas, however, unlike a growing Maracaibo depended for its ability to continue to grow upon an expanding
national market. Maracaibo as an outpost for an overseas market might have continued to grow simply because the demand for
oil was sufficient and growth in its region could have been attri-
buted largely to overseas development. Growth, of course, did
continue in Maracaibo though at a rate far lower than Caracas--
2% annually, as against 12% for the Capital region during the
1950's. Caracas was not producing oil but rather goods for the
domestic market. It needed thus a constantly expanding market
to continue its growth. And this expansion implied a need for
better transport.

There was moreover another important difference between the
kind of growth one expects to see in a dual economy and that
occurring in Caracas. The petroleum industry could only expand to those regions where additional subsoil deposits were to
be found. The industries being established in Caracas did not
really need the capital city location in any resource sense. Thus
though there may have been advantages at first in building a plant
where the demand to be satisfied is within easy reach, some of
that advantage is lost as growth proceeds.

For example, the supply of land for industrial development may
be a limiting factor. This was especially true in Caracas which
was after all located in a narrow valley where intensive sequent
occupance must eventually take place. That is to say, economic
activities requiring space are forced to compete for the limited
land resources available. This forces land use to be shifted
from less intensive to more intensive uses. Buildings become
taller. Population per city area rises. The rising cost of land
itself becomes an increasingly important fact in industrial location.

By the same token, labor costs rise. The paradox of this rise
in wages as well as in labor costs is that it was accompanied
in Caracas by the rapid growth of slums. But as has been demonstrated elsewhere[17] the key factor is the absorption rate as related to the actual availability of labor resources. Certainly, it
became true that for those industries in which productivity was
not rising fast, labor costs in the growing metropolis became
one more important element in a location decision.

TABLE I

Link Relatives of Manufacturing Value Added by Production, Various States, Venezuela, 1953-60

	Carabobo (Valencia)	Aragua (Maracay)	Distrito Federal (Caracas)	Miranda (Caracas)	Zulia (Maracaibo)	Lara (Barquisimeto)
1953	114.4	129.0	113.8	111.9	100.9	95.2
1954	125.1	110.5	111.2	93.8	118.1	93.2
1955	122.5	108.5	110.2	100.0	107.4	105.7
1956	108.2	111.2	110.1	103.9	107.7	103.4
1957	118.8	120.2	106.1	124.6	117.6	118.4
1958	108.7	130.0	110.5	102.8	87.7	104.7
1959	140.0	118.4	131.4	118.1	118.4	122.4
1960	105.8	109.8	103.1	100.0	85.8	144.2
Average Growth Rate	18%	17%	12%	7%	2%	9%

Source: Elaboration of production indexes from Memoria, Banco Central de Venezuela, 1961.

Comment: The period covered is too short to reveal more than the beginning impact of the highway. It is significant to note, however, that growth along the highway was not as greatly affected by the depression of the revolution as was Caracas and the metropolitan area or Maracaibo--the center of the petroleum industry. Also significant is that Barquisimeto, which lies east of Maracaibo and which was brought closer to Caracas by the highway, actually recorded a substantial gain in 1960.

The stage was being set for a spillover of economic activity
from Caracas. The effect of the decision to build highways
to increase the markets available to Caracas would be mani-
fold. Not only could goods produced in Caracas move out to
the oil regions as well as to older agricultural areas, but those
industries faced with rising land and labor costs could move out
into better locations. This process already observable by the
early 1950's had become well established late in the 1950's.

The movement of industries spilling out of the crowded Caracas
Valley into new zones implied also a movement of entrepreneurs.
The apparent tendency in a developing area is for there to be a
clustering of businessmen about the newer industries,[18] so much
so that the reward for business ability falls sharply at later
stages of growth. Some of these entrepreneurs will try their
fortunes in new zones as they open up.

Capital, too, tends to have a falling rate of return in growth
areas. And unless new and additional uses are found for the
flow of savings within the city, or growth area, there is an almost inevitable tendency for these funds to flow elsewhere. [19]
The opening up of new developmental areas constitutes a significant attraction. And here again in contrast to the dual economy example, the elsewhere need not be other petroleum fields
within the nation or outside.

By the time it was necessary to make a decision about how or
whether to improve the transport facilities in the Aragua Valley,
growth had spread westward from Caracas into that valley. Part
of the reason for the spread westward can be spelled out in the
spillover argument being elaborated. But why westward? Why
not eastward into the valleys around Guatire and Guarenas? Why
not in the more immediate vicinity of the oil and iron mining
centers? This requires a look at the highway and railway network which had been developing during this period.

Such a look reveals at once that the first major transport decisions in the country involved an attempt to connect the distant oil fields with the capital by land. The Maracaibo-Caracas
routes lay along the Aragua Valley. Likewise, the cheapest
direct route to the llanos lay through the Aragua Valley as well.
That is to say, once the growth points had emerged there were
distinct geographical advantages in the location of the Aragua
Valley.

The Growth of the Aragua Valley

The Aragua Valley contains two Venezuelan states, Aragua and Carabobo. Their capital cities, Maracay and Valencia, respectively, are the economic centers in the valley. Maracay had grown from an estimated population of about 30,000 in 1940 to around 160,000 in 1963. The growth of Valencia during the same period was from about 50,000 to almost 250,000. Corresponding growth has occurred in the states themselves. In general, these population growth rates were significantly faster than those in the nation.

The road under study goes south from Caracas and then turns west into the Aragua Valley. Tejerias is the first point on the highway in the valley and lies almost due south of Caracas. Between Caracas and Tejerias was a three-to four-lane undivided highway which, while a good basic highway in excellent condition, reaches nearly 7,000 feet and rises through substantial grades before it descends to the connection at Tejerias. It has been replaced by an expressway of the same general characteristics of the Tejerias-Valencia autopista which runs from an extension of the Caracas freeway system at Coche to connect with the Aragua Valley expressway somewhat east of the current toll station at Tejerias. The continuing improvement in the quality of transport services provided the Aragua Valley with lowering transport costs.

We know that during the decade of the 1950's, economic growth was faster in the Aragua Valley than in the Caracas Valley. We can measure this growth in terms of manufacturing indexes, of construction indexes, of bank clearances, of use of electrical energy as well as in terms of regional value added by manufacture. In fact, whereas Aragua and Carabobo represented some 7.8% of total manufacturing output in 1955, by 1962, these two states accounted for 14% of such production.

We know, too, that it was in durable goods particularly that Aragua Valley industry was growing. And in metal products, machinery, vehicles, and the like, very high growth rates were recorded in this region, in excess--on an average--of 33% a year in Carabobo, for example. Nondurables, too, gained in the Caracas region. And what is interesting is that the chemical industry grew many times faster in Carabobo than in Zulia, the state of which Maracaibo is capital. Put it another way, we can

establish without question that growth when it began in the Aragua Valley was fast. Moreover, we can show that growth continued even during the depression produced in part by the revolution against the dictator, Perez Jimenez, at rates that outdis-
tanced Caracas.

In so doing, however, we are confirming the existence of a demand for transport and providing the basis for explaining the
high benefit-cost ratios obtained by the investment in the autopista. But we are not explaining what the development impact
of the highway considered apart from the growth context might
have been. Did the highway produce effects which are visible
and which can be measured which would not have been there in
the absence of this particular kind of transport investment? Did
the highway do things that a railway might not have done? Did
the character and location of the highway produce results that
other right-of-way decisions might not have produced? Even more
generally, can the nature and direction of Venezuelan economic
development be explained in any way in terms of the impact of
this highway investment? Because the answer to each of these
questions is affirmative, what is otherwise a routine examination of benefit-cost relations becomes an exercise in the analysis
of development benefits of significance for developing nations.

Industrial Response to the Autopista

It has been established that the autopista had direct effects on
the costs of moving things through the Aragua Valley. Moreover, we know that industrialization proceeded rapidly in the
cities of the valley. It is useful therefore to examine in some detail the connection between the change in transport costs and the
nature of industrialization in a number of Aragua urban places.
This takes us necessarily into an analysis of changes in land use
patterns.

Before growth began to spill over into the Aragua Valley, the
principal economic activities were agricultural and naturally so
given the excellent land and climate available in this region. The
crops grown tended to make an extensive rather than an intensive
use of the land so that value produced per hectare was relatively
low. Cotton, corn, rice, and cattle were the basic elements of
the agricultural economy. Maracay was the nation's principal
slaughtering center as well as an important textile producer. It

TABLE II

Value Added by Manufacture: Venezuela, Certain States, 1952-60
(Constant 1957 Prices)
(Bolivars, add 000,000)

	Carabobo	Aragua	Distrito Federal	Miranda	Zulia	Lara
1952	58.2	32.8	473.6	168.3	135.8	272.9
1953	66.5	42.3	571.1	188.2	137.0	259.9
1954	83.2	46.7	599.1	176.5	161.8	242.2
1955	101.9	50.7	664.9	175.6	173.7	256.0
1956	110.3	56.4	705.3	182.3	178.2	264.4
1957	131.0	67.7	783.5	227.1	220.1	313.2
1958	142.5	88.0	865.9	223.5	192.9	328.0
1959	199.4	104.2	1,137.4	275.8	228.4	401.3
1960	211.1	114.4	1,175.2	275.7	195.9	578.8

Source: Elaborated from Jose M. Sucre, Estimacion Preliminar del Valor Agregado por Entidades Federales y por Sector Economico para 1960, Caracas, Corporacion Venezolana de Guayana, 1961, and from Memoria, Banco Central de Venezuela, 1961.

35

TABLE

III

Carabobo and Aragua States as a Per Cent of Total Manufacturing
Output in Venezuela, 1955-62

1955	7. 81
1957	9. 44
1958	10.07
1959	11.19
1961	12. 32
1962	14.00

Source: Elaborated from Jose M. Sucre, Estimacion Preliminar del Valor
Agregado por Entidades Federales y por Sector Economico para 1960, Caracas,
Corporacion Venezolana de Guayana, 1961, and from Memoria, Banco
Central de Venezuela, 1961.

TABLE IV

Industrial Production Indexes, Various Industries and States, Venezuela, 1960 (1953=100)

	Nation	Aragua	Carabobo	Distrito Federal	Miranda	Zulia	Lara
All Industries	216.6	270.6	317.2	218.1	146.5	143.0	222.7
Durable Goods	204.6	547.1	514.2	154.6	92.4	182.2	384.2
Wood Products	132.5	117.7	82.9	168.2	75.9	89.4	197.4
Rubber	324.6	–	1,648.6	423.0	105.4	–	–
Nonmetallic Minerals	143.7	178.2	125.8	106.5	87.2	159.1	545.2
Metal Products	659.1	2,401.9	–	194.9	50.6	2,296.9	136.6
Nondurables	218.4	245.0	287.5	232.5	164.5	95.9	221.4
Food	201.3	254.1	186.9	365.0	103.6	86.3	332.4
Beverages	206.6	–	279.6	179.6	163.5	170.2	203.9
Tobacco	239.0	214.0	–	208.0	–	67.6	–
Textiles	268.8	256.5	112.0	205.7	508.3	534.5	18,226.1
Clothing	180.5	238.7	–	–	233.3	–	–
Paper	618.9	–	1,794.9	267.0	1,018.3	9,850.0	–
Printing	220.0	–	–	–	–	–	–
Hides and Skins	214.5	1,596.9	151.0	131.7	1,462.3	65.3	306.2
Chemicals	218.0	162.8	827.0	157.9	266.9	127.6	1,622.8
Petroleum Products	203.6	–	–	–	–	–	–
Miscellaneous	482.6	592.6	–	1,480.3	–	133.9	736.6

Sources: Elaboration of industry data in Memoria, Banco Central de Venezuela, 1961, and unpublished bank reports.

Comment: Though these are relative and not absolute numbers, they did indicate clearly the changing pattern of industrial location along the route of the highway and confirm the visual appreciation of sequent occupance.

37

is no surprise therefore to find that in the city in 1940, the industrial land use revealed the nature of the surrounding valley's
economy.

On Map 1, Zone 1 covers that area of industries which pre-
existed the highway investment. Lying along the railway, there
are some textile mills (all of them multistory buildings), some
meat-processing plants along with a large cattle-handling and
slaughter-facility, and some tanning plants. Clearly, the
function of Maracay, apart from the governmental responsibilities assigned to it as the state's capital, was that of adding
value to the valley's agricultural produce so that it might sell
elsewhere in the nation as well as in the Aragua Valley.

Zone 2 lies along the Pan American Highway east and west of the
city. Here by the early 1950's were to be found cigarette manufacturing plants, food processing--canning of fruits and vegetables, corn flakes, and the like. In addition, there were small
plants devoted to the repair of automobiles and trucks, as well
as the manufacture of some parts--axles, springs, piston rings,
and the like. Zone 2 revealed an intensification of the value
added process as well as a shift in the surrounding area to more
valuable crops or at least the obtaining of more value from crops
already in production. On the map, it is apparent that the effect
of the introduction of such additional activities along the Pan
American Highway had tended to stretch the city from its colonial
rectangular form.

When we turn to Zone 3, we see for the first time activities which
do not depend either upon the agricultural production of the valley
or upon the transport industry itself. Here are metal-working
plants making machinery and parts for use in a wide variety of
industries located all over the country. Here, too, is a paper
plant along with much bigger canning facilities, a concrete pipe
plant and very modern single-story textile plants. Moreover, unlike almost all the industries seen in Zones 1 and 2, many of these
plants are foreign owned and in most cases branches of overseas
companies. This zone lies just north of the right of way of the
new expressway. It essentially represents an unplanned response
to the transport facility in much the same way as Zones 1 and 2.

Zone 4, however, is a planned industrial park. It lies south of
the highway in an area at some distance from other urban develop-

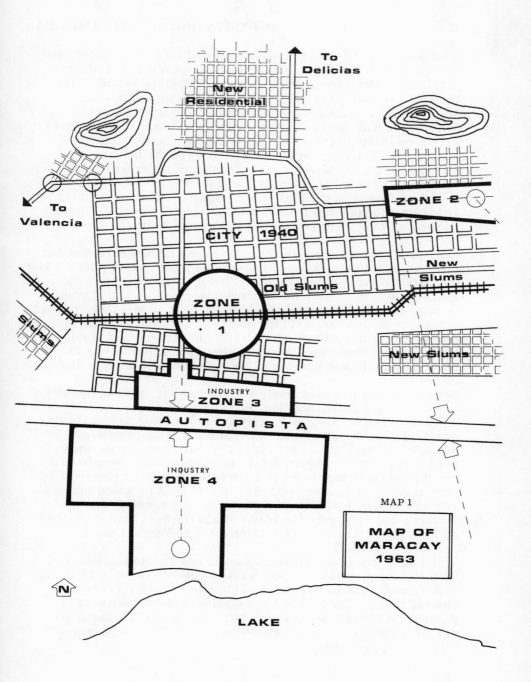

To Delicias

New Residential

To Valencia

CITY 1940

ZONE 2

New Slums

Old Slums

ZONE · 1

Slums

New Slums

INDUSTRY ZONE 3

AUTOPISTA

INDUSTRY ZONE 4

MAP 1

MAP OF MARACAY 1963

N

LAKE

ment and required the provision of special highways, water, and sewage as well as bus service. Here are pharmaceutical, apparel, specialty papergoods and container plants, and other industries, almost all of which represent activities for which Maracay has no particular geographical advantage except in comparison with land and labor costs in Caracas. These plants have been located here when they could have been located at other points in the nation because relative to the market they propose to supply, Maracay had advantages. It must not be overlooked in addition that Maracay, because it was in 1940 not significantly different in cultural attainments, in standard of living, and in growth potential from Caracas, needed only the transport investment to exploit the labor and land cost differences.

Even more dramatic are the changes which have occurred at the terminal of the autopista in Valencia (Map 2). Just beyond the last toll gate and lying to the south well before the entrance to the old city, is a vast new planned industrial park. While it would be interesting to trace, as we did in the case of Maracay, through sequent occupance analysis the nature of the industrial changes and the shifts in land use, the park is the predominant feature of the Valencia economy. Larger in area than Valencia was in 1940, the park clearly was planned to take advantage of the new highway.

Here are the major automobile-assembling facilities in the nation. Here, too, are paint, plastics, and chemical plants, as well as metal processing of every variety. Soap, rubber tire, and other products of rubber, building materials including cement give examples of the kinds of activities that have been established here. The park was begun before the highway was completed, and this helps in part to explain the industrial boom clearly evident in the statistics before 1958. But it must be added that the city had a further advantage which gives it a decided edge over Maracay and even over Caracas. It has the best harbor available on Venezuela's north coast adjacent to it at Puerto Cabello.

To be sure, the road between Valencia and Puerto Cabello was, until the completion of the expressway between them, a nightmare of a highway reaching above 7, 000 feet in the passes over the coastal range. The highway and a railway shared the narrow passes and where towns were to be found, all three shared the narrow valley floors under conditions that called for maximum ingenuity in land usage.

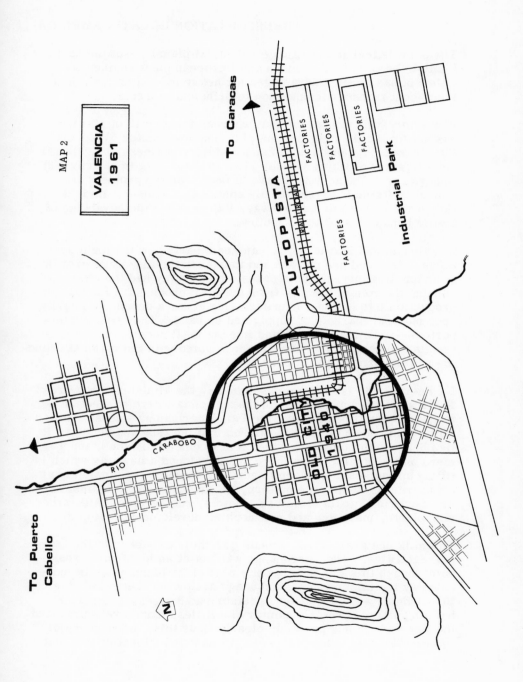

MAP 2

VALENCIA
1961

To Caracas

AUTOPISTA

RAILROAD

FACTORIES

FACTORIES

FACTORIES

FACTORIES

Industrial Park

OLD CITY 1940

RIO CARABOBO

To Puerto Cabello

N

41

The point is that in long-range industrial planning--of the sort
likely to be done by American and European plant engineers--
Valencia had distinct advantages for heavy industry once it had
a low-cost transport connection to principal markets.

It is interesting to observe that whereas the growth of Maracay
has not forced the development of a new town center, Valencia
like Caracas has begun to form subsidiary business and cultural
centers, some of which already rival the old plaza in activity and
importance. Maracay will have to face soon the problem of
traffic on its main arteries. By contrast, because of its location at the end of the expressway, Valencia has the advantage of
traffic bypasses north and southwest of the city.

In Valencia and Maracay, we can see clearly how the highway
affected the land use pattern and therefore the industrial growth
of an existing city. In both cases, the highway had the effect of
shifting the role of the city from that of a processor of local
production into national manufacturing centers dependent heavily
upon national markets of supply and demand. They became im-
porters--in both a national and international sense--of raw materials and parts. They became integrated with the national economy and important growth points.

La Encrucijada is the name assigned by the Ministerio de Obras
Publicas to the interchange on the autopista where connection is
made between this highway, the Pan American as well as Route 2
which leads down through the llanos into the Guayana country. It
lies between the old market towns of Cagua on the south and Turmero on the north. Here there has developed a new city which is
filling up the space between Cagua and Turmero. Completely unplanned in its land usage pattern, La Encrucijada is a jumble of
new factories, grain elevators, motels, restaurants, milk-proces-
sing plants, markets, and new housing developments (Map 3).

The milk and grain developments owe their existence to the transport facilities. The interchange was set at an ideal bulk breaking
point though this was surely not a part of its planning as is indicated by the mishmash of land usage around it. Likewise, the
light industry--lamps, tiles, prefabricated stressed concrete
building units, porcelain sanitary facilities, hardware items, and
the like--which has grown up clearly finds this, the first major
intersection on the highway west of Caracas, a location of great

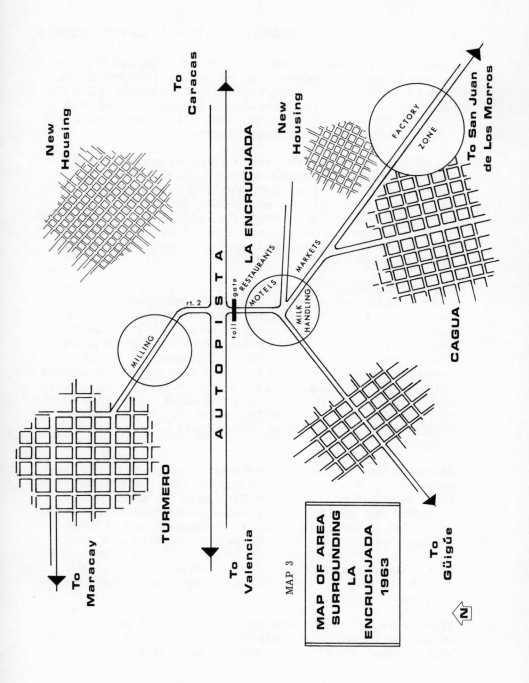

New Housing

To Caracas

LA ENCRUCIJADA

New Housing

To San Juan de Los Morros

FACTORY ZONE

AUTOPISTA

rt. 2

toll gate

RESTAURANTS

MOTELS

MARKETS

MILK HANDLING

MILLING

CAGUA

TURMERO

To Valencia

To Maracay

MAP 3

To Güigüe

MAP OF AREA SURROUNDING LA ENCRUCIJADA 1963

N

43

advantage since from it almost all sections of the nation can be
reached by paved highway without the doubling back necessary
from Caracas or Maracay or Valencia. Significantly, all of the
new industries here are Venezuelan owned and managed, and
many are obviously activities which began in Caracas and were
forced to seek land for expansion elsewhere.

In addition, the presence of truck terminals, motels, restaurants indicates the advantages that this place has for the transport industry itself. Here there was no pre-existing city with
its narrow colonial streets, no buildings to tear down, and no
restriction as to land use. While the result is not a pretty one,
the air of constant activity--even late at night--is evidence of
the net benefit this crossroads represents for the regional and
national economies.

The spelling out of the sequent occupance pattern in the Valley
is not complete without some looking at the agricultural land use
pattern as well. Corn and cotton have been replaced by sugar,
especially in the eastern reaches of the valley. In the west, vegetables for canning have pushed rice and corn out of the valley.
Chicken farming--eggs and broilers--following the American
model makes intensive use of land near each of the intersections
of the highway. This process of shifting production has in part
been aided by irrigation of the upper areas of the Western Llanos
all reached by highways extending either from La Encrucijada or
from Valencia so that rice and cotton could and did move to
cheaper land.

All this helps us to see the development benefits in their proper
perspective. It is clear that the highway made possible the shifting of economic activities from Caracas to the Aragua Valley. To
the extent that such activities could be carried on cheaper in the
valley than in the city of Caracas--cheaper because of lower land
and labor costs--there was a net gain in the purchasing power
of consumer incomes and/or industrial profits. The fact, however, that consumer prices remained stable during the 1950's
and into the 1960's suggests that at the very least consumers did
not lose by this shift.

There were, however, some activities which did not take place
in Caracas and which probably could not have taken place there
which we find establishing themselves in the Valley. These are

the metal-working industries and similar activities in the building materials field which in the production processes emit smoke
and fumes which could not be tolerated in the narrow confines of
the Caracas Valley.   These present clear evidence of a net gain
to the valley which is also a net gain to the national economy.
But these are industries which would have had to be established
somewhere.   The highway made possible their development in
the Aragua Valley.   Likewise the shifts in agricultural production in the valley are part of a national development pattern in
which location of the activity is the consequence of the state of
development as well as of the availability of space.

Were there any activities which permitted an important substitution and thus a saving of foreign exchange?   For a nation with a
heavy export surplus, largely because of oil, this may not appear
to be an important question.   Nonetheless, it is certainly possible
that even these generous funds might be more effectively used.
The evidence provided by a study of foreign trade statistics reveals not only the expected shift from a heavy early emphasis on
consumer goods imports to raw materials but a gradual decline
in the relative importance of capital goods imports.

It was in transportation equipment, construction equipment,
durable consumer goods as well as in foodstuffs that imports
fell off sharply.   But these are precisely the areas in which the
Aragua Valley production boomed.   In 1962, transport equipment
import quantum was 82% of the 1948 level and less than 25% of
the 1957 level.   Construction equipment imports were down to
27% of the level for 1948, but raw materials and parts imports
were at 331% in physical volume terms of the immediate postwar levels.   Durable goods for consumers were down to 70%
of the earlier imports despite the growing sale of such goods in
all urban centers.   And by 1963, President Betancourt was able
to announce that Venezuela was self-sufficient in a wide range
of foodstuffs--eggs, milk, butter, meats, potatoes, vegetables,
rice.   All of these shifts in important elements of the import
picture for Venezuela are, as we have seen, directly related to
changes in the Aragua Valley.   To the extent that the highway
made possible these changes, it must be credited with the value
of development benefits arising.

Thus we are enabled to see the meaning of the statistics available
though we cannot spell out in definitive terms the exact measure

TABLE V

Imports: Index Numbers, 1949-62 (1948=100)

	Transport Equipment		Construction Equipment		Raw Materials		Food Products		Durable Consumer Goods	
	Q*	V*	Q	V	Q	V	Q	V	Q	V
1949	-	-	-	-	66.4	144.7	121.6	88.4	109.0	24.3
1950	79.6	110.5	65.2	80.4	77.5	119.7	134.1	78.6	97.4	22.9
1951	77.7	116.6	81.0	108.8	91.9	124.2	144.5	79.2	100.0	24.3
1952	119.4	91.9	65.9	164.2	92.4	128.4	120.4	87.8	99.3	26.5
1953	118.6	99.4	54.6	170.6	113.9	117.0	127.1	83.9	107.5	24.2
1954	109.2	127.5	57.0	156.0	140.3	113.2	129.1	84.6	110.6	25.2
1955	140.9	116.2	70.1	163.6	144.1	113.4	130.6	91.4	122.9	25.1
1956	120.5	133.7	86.7	210.6	154.5	116.0	131.9	89.8	128.1	23.9
1957	261.6	113.9	180.7	229.4	193.4	116.6	106.9	94.9	59.8	47.1
1958	163.5	147.5	99.4	224.6	207.1	122.5	113.9	69.5	62.8	46.4
1959	200.5	152.5	62.3	222.1	308.4	98.4	101.5	193.2	107.2	57.2
1960	125.8	159.6	38.2	223.5	275.7	93.2	76.6	133.7	80.5	56.8
1961	94.3	207.8	23.9	251.2	288.5	102.0	82.2	114.9	68.5	73.0
1962	81.9	237.2	26.6	244.7	330.5	108.5	57.5	152.9	70.2	78.0

*Q = Quantum; V = Value

46

TABLE V (contd.)

Index Numbers: Imports, Terms of Trade and Capacity to Import
(1948=100)

	Import Quantum	Import Value	Terms of Trade	Capacity to Import
1949	106.60	85.34	106.14	101.40
1950	81.13	71.20	121.24	132.04
1951	92.45	81.21	106.37	134.59
1952	83.49	90.48	103.31	143.79
1953	63.68	97.83	115.64	153.64
1954	98.11	109.28	113.57	163.53
1955	106.60	116.02	115.96	189.50
1956	117.92	133.81	104.64	200.61
1957	176.89	198.86	96.83	203.85
1958	141.50	170.23	100.17	199.51
1959	137.26	167.99	81.35	182.85
1960	106.60	126.42	84.09	191.45
1961	101.88	125.34	75.57	169.60
1962	107.08	139.00	64.37	156.39

Source: Various Memoria, Banco Central de Venezuela.

of the development benefit. The highway made possible the
continuing of a growth process begun in the oil fields and later
centralized in Caracas. It helped channel the inevitable industrial spillover from Caracas into the valley. It integrated the
valley into the national development by reducing the differentials
which had previously existed. This integration was not simply
a geographical one but rather a process by which the valley became a direct and important contributor to the growth of the
national product. And the highway thus made possible the spread
of the Venezuelan growth process.

In this chapter, then, we see that a highway investment can bring
about a situation in which the spread effects are clearly greater
than the backwash effects. [20] The importance of this lesson for
Peru--at a much earlier stage in economic development with its
growth largely concentrated in Lima--for example, cannot be
overlooked. Highway planning can thus become a part of planning for the more equitable distribution of the benefits of economic growth.

Now to summarize the development benefits spelled out in a
general way in this part, we have devised a table. Table VI
differs from the others in not specifying values. Rather what it
does is to outline the general nature of the benefits which are the
result of pushing out the economic frontiers of Venezuela consequent upon the investment in the Valencia-Tejerias highway. These
are the benefits not taken into account when a reckoning of time,
shippers' and user cost savings is made. Because they are more
basic than the former, they give an idea of the result for development strategy of highway investment rather than just a measure
of investment returns.

The benefits spelled out in development terms are essentially
gross in nature. That is to say, they do not take into account
negative changes which have occurred elsewhere in Venezuela.
We have however netted out the difference between regional and
national benefits. The measures spelled out establish that a good
share of the gross gain to the Aragua Valley was in fact a net benefit for the nation since many new activities that might not otherwise have been located in Venezuela--had the location choice been
limited to Caracas--are in production. Note also that the declin-
ing terms of trade made imperative the effective use of foreign
exchange and an adequate policy of import substitution, this despite the continuing high level of foreign-exchange earnings. Thus,

TABLE VI
Summary of Economic Development Benefits Attributable
Directly or Indirectly to the Tejerias-Valencia Autopista,
as of Early 1963

Local/Regional Economic Development

1.   The rise in the relative economic importance of Aragua
     and Carabobo
          Though obviously not all this rise can be attributed
          to the highway since the process had begun before it
          was finished, it is possible to argue that in the ab-
          sence of the highway, the process might have stopped
          or slowed down and the potential growth might have
          been shifted elsewhere. Thus that growth over the
          national average coming after the highway may be
          assigned to the highway.

2.   Rise in Value Productivity of Regional Factors of Production
          The sequent occupance process shows how for land,
          and especially for urban land, there was a shift in
          land usages from less intensive to more intensive and
          therefore more productive employments. Though it
          was impossible to trace the same process in labor
          and capital employments, an essentially analogous
          process was visible there. Since discounted value
          productivity may be used as an index of wealth, we
          can assign to the highway particularly those increases
          in land values--if we knew them--along the right-of-
          way. Similarly, increases in the value of labor and
          in its income could be so assigned.

National Economic Development

1.   The Spread of Economic Development from center of con-
     centration to "new" areas
          Venezuelan economic planners like those elsewhere
          in the developing world have been concerned with the
          tendency for industry and therefore the benefits of
          economic development to be concentrated in the na-
          tion's capital. To the extent that this highway made
          possible "spread effects" that must be chalked up as
          a development benefit.

49

2.   Reduction on Dependence on Imports and the Savings
     in Foreign Exchange
         To the extent that the highway permitted the intro-
         duction of economic activities that could not have
         been located in Caracas and which substituted for
         imports, there was a benefit. The direct and im-
         mediate measure of the benefit is the release of for-
         eign exchange for the purchase of items thought to
         be more necessary to development. It should be
         pointed out though that this may also mean a less
         flexible import budget since the activities being set
         up in the Aragua Valley tend more and more to re-
         quire essential parts, assemblies and raw materials.

3.   Prevention of Possible Cost Rises
         The increasing concentration of economic activity in
         Caracas would have meant rising land prices and labor
         wages. To the extent that these were avoided--and the
         evidence available in the fact of no increase in the
         cost-of-living and wholesale price indexes--there was
         a benefit from the building of the highway. The im-
         portance of avoiding the structural basis for an in-
         flationary spiral must not be underemphasized since
         this is a major element in the inflations of Chile, Ar-
         gentina, and Brazil.

4.   Better Integration of the National Economy
         The value of economic integration is not easy to mea-
         sure, but some of its elements may be appraised by
         an examination of the flow of commerce as indicated
         by the origin and destination study taken the year after
         the first unit of the highway was installed. As observed
         in the text of the case study, the Aragua Valley cities be-
         came to a greater extent than anticipated "national" pro-
         duction centers. Whatever disadvantages the "dual
         economy" may have for a nation, this highway was one
         important step in avoiding it for Venezuela.

Comment: Because of the nature of the statistics available, it
was not possible to assign specific values to these benefits. Yet
some appreciation of their possible magnitudes may be gained
from the tables in this chapter.

there was also a net benefit in terms of development flexibility arising from being able to find areas which permitted continuing import substitution.

What this part has indicated is that the needs which led to the decision to build the highway were those arising out of the development process in Venezuela. Though the highway was not itself a prime mover in this development process, it did play an important role as a channeler of the process and moreover did permit it to continue. Its essential justification then consists in its enabling role rather than in its propulsive role.

SUMMARY AND CONCLUSIONS

A frequent criticism of the Venezuelan highway construction program is that there has been too much emphasis upon impressive monuments and that therefore less has been available for more modest but more necessary projects. In this case study of an autopista in the Aragua Valley, we see that the Ministry of Public Works made its decision to build this very expensive facility in terms of demand-and-supply reasoning. Choosing among the alternatives, the Ministry apparently made that decision likely to yield the greatest benefit. We have seen that the direct benefits accruing to the users of the highway were high. But we have also seen that the development benefits in the context of the Aragua Valley and of the nation were also substantial.

To be sure, Venezuela has had the funds available to be able to make a massive response to the demand situations and thus perhaps to achieve maximum benefit results. It has not had the cruel choice facing so many nations in the process of economic development where limited funds must be spread in small amounts among many projects with consequent limited results everywhere.

The over-all effect of such heavy transport investments has been to lower significantly the social and total costs of transport in Venezuela. Transport, for example, as a per cent of the Gross Domestic Product fell from over 5% in 1950 to around 3.4% by 1961. From 1955 through 1961, the average output-capital ratio for transport fell from 0.23 to 0.11. Meanwhile, the marginal capital-output ratio rose irregularly from 0.94 to 1.24.

Thus, there was a general tendency for higher marginal capital-output ratios to be associated with lower percentage relations between GDP and transport industry output. This may be
taken to be general evidence of the over-all benefit of the transport program since such highway investments as the Aragua
Valley expressway--the major element in the late 1950's national
highway program--greatly increased the productivity of the transport industry.

The one general conclusion from this case study which is applicable to the problem of the relation of highway investments and
the economic development process is that massive transport decisions in the "right" place produce massive results. That right
place is determined in terms of existing and future demand for
and supply of transport. But the fact that these "right places"
are themselves already growth points need not necessarily lead
to more concentration and may in fact aid the spillover process.

The secondary conclusion is that massive transport investment
in the right place tends to create other "right" places--the example of Valencia--which in turn become growth points creating
need for further transport and thus the development process goes
on changing the economic landscape. Transport investments,
then, are strategic to a dynamic growth process. That much is
evident from this case study. For other case studies must remain the answer to the question as to whether massive transport
investments can create growth and development in the absence of
a known demand.

APPENDIX A

The Highway Transport Resources of Venezuela

There were in 1961, some 34,000 kilometers of highway in Venezuela. Nearly 27,000 kilometers of this system were numbered highways and therefore regarded part of the national system. About 45% of this system is regularly maintained.

TABLE A-I
Roads in Venezuela, 1961

Types of Roads	Km	Km Maintained	% Maintained
Superhighways	128	128	100
Paved highways	8,438	8,438	100
Macadamized highways	9,849	3,640	37
Graveled highways	8,408		
Numbered highways	26,823	12,206	45
Dirt/Graded highways	6,096		
Tracks	1,305		
Total all highways	34,224		

Source: Memoria, Banco Central de Venezuela, 1961.

Six types of highways as classified by the Ministry of Public Works were being or had been constructed as indicated by the following table.

TABLE A-II
Description and Classification of Highways in Venezeula

Type AA   Superhighway for four lanes of traffic. Estimated average costs per km, Bs 1,250,000.

Type A   Average daily traffic of 1,500-5,000 vehicles; average design speed 100 kmph in hilly terrain and some-

cont'd.

what higher in flat; 7.3 meter paved surface on an
11 meter grade; 10 cm of asphalt concrete wearing
surface over a 15 cm crushed rock or gravel base
on a sand and gravel sub-base of normally 22.5 cm.
Minimum right-of-way 60 meters, estimated average cost per km Bs 625,000 per km. Paved shoulders
1.85 meters.

Type B   Average daily traffic of 600-1,500 vehicles, average
design 80 kmph in hilly terrain and somewhat higher
in flat. 7.3 meter paved surface on an 11 meter
grade. 10 cm of asphalt concrete wearing surface
over a 15 cm crushed rock or gravel base, on a sand
and gravel sub-base of normally 22.5 cm. Minimum
right-of-way 60 meters. Estimated average cost per
km, Bs 500,000.

Type C   Average daily traffic of 200-600 vehicles; average
design speed 60 kmph in hilly terrain and somewhat
higher in flat terrain, 6.5 meter paved surface on a
10 meter grade. 2 cm of a bituminous macadam surface covering a 30 cm stone and gravel foundation.
Minimum right-of-way 60 meters. Estimated average
cost per km, Bs 290,000.

Type D   Average daily traffic of 50-200 vehicles; average design speed 40 kmph in hilly terrain and somewhat
higher in flat; 6 meter graveled surface on an 8 meter
grade, 15 cm thick. No paved surface but drained.
Minimum right-of-way 30 meters. Average estimated
cost per km, Bs 150,000.

Type E   Average daily traffic of 50 vehicles or less, suitable
for provincial farm roads, average design speed, 35
kmph in hilly terrain and somewhat higher in flat.
Grade 4 meters wide with turnouts for passing. Minimum right-of-way 30 meters. Estimated construction
cost per km, Bs 50,000.

Note: Prices refer to 1959 contracts.

Source: Banco Central de Venezuela, IBRD.

In 1961, there were 275,000 automobiles and more than 97,000 trucks in use along with 6,500 buses. This was the fourth largest vehicle fleet in Latin America, and given the relative size of the population and area, the highway transport resources in Venezuela were substantially larger than in other Latin American countries, in relative terms.

TABLE A-III
Vehicle Fleet--Venezuela

Automobiles	1959	1961	1962
Private	209,447	242,960	249,492
Taxis, long distance	29,548	31,450	30,413
	238,995	274,410	279,905
Buses	6,800	6,456	6,433
Trucks	93,305	97,318	107,384
	338,100	378,184	393,722

Source: Memoria, Banco Central de Venezuela, 1962.

Vehicle acquisition costs are slightly higher in Venezuela than in the United States though substantially lower than in most of Latin America. For example, trucks in terms of bolivares per ton of payload ranged in 1959 from Bs 4,700 to Bs 5,700 ($1,600 to $1,900). Automobiles ranged up to 25% above U. S. prices. Fuel costs are very low with regular grade gasoline selling in 1959 at 14 centimos a liter, or between 11 and 12 cents a gallon. In general truck operating costs are moderate.

TABLE A-IV
Truck Operating Costs (centimos/ton/kilometer)

Truck Capacity (tons)	7.8	11.4	15.9	21.0	23.5
Load Factor (per cent)	70.0	55.0	50.0	42.0	40.0
Labor Costs	6.5	5.7	4.8	4.5	4.6
Capital Costs	6.1	6.4	6.6	7.0	7.3
Total Costs	12.6	12.1	11.4	11.5	11.9

Source: Soberman, Cost of Road Transportation in Venezuela, Corporacion Venezolana de Guayana, 1962.

By combining vehicle operating costs for both trucks and automobiles, we have worked out the cost schedule for all vehicles
for each type of highway for 1962. This is presented in Table A-V.

TABLE A-V
Vehicle Operating Costs per Vehicle-Kilometer, 1962
by Type of Highway, Venezuela

Type of Highway	Operating Cost (Bs.)	Actual Traffic, 1962
AA	0.19	14,133
A	0.25	9,171
B	0.35	1,844
C	0.55	1,300
D	0.76	650

Sources: Traffic reports of Ministry of Public Works, cost estimates from Banco Central, IBRD.

These data would indicate a substantial reduction in operating costs
for lower to higher design highways in Venezuela. Of similar
import are data elaborated for construction costs as presented in
Table A-VI.

TABLE A-VI
Schedule of Annualized Highway Construction Costs
(By Type of Highway Showing the Changes in Costs
Allocated per Vehicle Km Resulting From Shift
From One Type of Highway to the Next Lower)

Type Highway	Annual Equivalent Cost of Construction Bs/km 30 yrs., 8%	Maintenance Cost per km	Total Annual Cost per km	Change in Cost
AA	293,761	51,000	344,761	0.07
A	242,288	14,500	256,788	0.08
B	44,415	10,500	54,915	0.09
C	25,761	6,100	31,861	0.07
D	13,325	3,000	16,325	0.07
E	4,442	1,000	5,442	

Sources: Elaboration of data from Ministry of Public Works,
Banco Central de Venezuela, IBRD.

Here there would appear to be something akin to constant return to scale as traffic and design standards increase, for the costs of construction and maintenance per vehicle change within a very narrow range and possibly not at all as these variables move up in value.

The implication of both of these sets of data is that it is cheaper to build high design facilities when traffic is heavy.

APPENDIX B
Origin and Destination Study

An origin and desitnation survey was conducted in Venezuela in June, 1959, by the Army using among other points the alacabalas set up as check points along the highways. The information contained in the following tables refers to the freight movements by truck in the Aragua Valley and from principal points along the route of the Valencia-Tejerias autopista. This survey, however, refers to all highways, rather than just the autopista, in the valley. However, Tables B-I, B-II, and B-III present only traffic movements along the Valencia-Tejerias route. Table B-IV summarizes all freight movements from Maracay and Valencia by all routes.

TABLE B-I
Valencia

Origin and Destination Survey, June, 1959--Freight
Movement by Truck, Highways in the Aragua Valley

| | Freight in Tons | | |
	East	West	Total
Cagua-Turmero	560. 6	616. 6	1,177. 2
El Consejo	-	-	469. 6
Guacara	2,282. 6	34. 9	317. 5
La Victoria	71. 6	347. 9	419. 5
Las Tejerias	0	53. 2	54. 2
Maracay	5,620. 4	2,786.1	8,406. 5
Valencia	2,834. 6	0	2,834. 6
Total	9,369. 8	3,838. 7	13,678.1

cont'd.

TABLE B-I, continued

	Freight in Tons Km		
	East	West	Total
Cagua-Turmero	176.530	134.342	310.872
El Consejo	-	-	152.628
Guacara	73.080	8.567	81.647
La Victoria	16.017	83.651	99.668
Las Tejerias	0	17.458	17.458
Maracay	1,175.150	829.991	2,005.141
Valencia	782.232	0	782.232
Total	2,234.009	1,074.009	3,449.646

One surprising conclusion emerging from this survey is the relative unimportance of the movements into Caracas and the extent, therefore, to which the Aragua Valley cities had already become suppliers of the national rather than simply the metropolitan economy.

TABLE B-II
Venezuela

Origin and Destination Survey, June, 1959-- Freight in Truck by Percentage of Total Shipment in Ton Km, Aragua Valley (Refers Only to Movements Valencia-Las Tejerias)

Destination	Origin						
	Cagua-Turmero	El Consejo	Guacara	La Victoria	Las Tejerias	Maracay	Valencia
Maracay	1.66	-	-	0.81	1.95	0.01	-
Valencia	-	13.16	-	10.82	-	1.02	0.20
Cagua	-	-	-	-	-	0.36	0.31
Barcelona	15.39	-	2.69	6.40	-	6.25	15.13
Barquisimeto	3.94	-	0.81	5.33	-	2.37	-
Maracaibo	19.31	-	0.80	17.24	39.12	8.96	-
Cuidad Bolivar	-	-	-	5.31	-	3.61	12.75
Cumana	-	-	-	8.80	-	7.62	3.89
Puerto Cabello	0.97	-	-	0.81	-	2.81	-
Guarenas	0.23	-	-	-	-	0.13	0.41
Guatire	-	-	-	-	-	-	0.10
San Cristobal	-	5.45	-	3.30	28.73	10.89	-
Merida	1.63	-	-	-	-	0.28	-
Maturin	11.68	-	-	2.86	-	9.09	-
Caracas	7.39	-	5.27	3.83	-	12.87	21.04
	62.20	18.61	9.57	71.51	69.80	66.27	53.83
Others	37.80	81.39	90.43	28.49	30.20	33.73	46.17
Total	100.00	100.00	100.00	100.00	100.00	100.00	100.00

59

TABLE B-III
Venezuela

Origin and Destination Survey, June, 1959--Freight Movements in Truck by Percentage of Total Shipments in Tons, Aragua Valley (Refers Only to Movements Valencia-Las Tejerias)

Destination	Origin						
	Cagua-Turmero	El Consejo	Guacara	La Victoria	Las Tejerias	Maracay	Valencia
Maracay	25.46	-	-	5.64	11.65	0.20	-
Valencia	-	42.86	-	28.72	-	4.42	2.92
Cagua	-	-	3.75	-	-	4.79	1.21
Barcelona	8.24	-	1.25	2.86	-	3.02	7.78
Barquisimetro	3.92	-	0.91	4.29	-	2.26	-
Maracaibo	7.62	-	-	6.03	18.79	3.31	-
Cuidad Bolivar	-	-	-	1.90	-	1.37	5.21
Cumana	-	-	-	3.71	-	3.08	1.70
Puerto Cabello	1.95	-	-	11.17	-	6.37	-
Guarenas	0.68	-	-	-	-	0.27	0.56
Guatire	-	-	-	-	-	-	0.14
San Cristobal	-	2.12	-	0.95	11.27	3.28	-
Merida	0.68	-	-	-	-	0.11	-
Maturin	3.74	-	-	0.95	-	2.74	-
Caracas	23.04	-	9.22	11.68	-	27.70	35.22
	75.33	44.98	15.13	77.90	41.71	62.92	54.74
Others	24.67	55.02	84.87	22.10	58.29	37.08	45.74
Total	100.00	100.00	100.00	100.00	100.00	100.00	100.1

TABLE B-IV
Venezuela

Origin and Destination Survey, June, 1959--All
Freight from Maracay and Valencia in Truck by
All Highways

Destination	Origin			
	Maracay		Valencia	
	Tons	Ton Km	Tons	Ton Km
Maracay	0.20	0.01	4.40	0.88
Valencia	4.41	1.01	1.00	0.06
Cagua	4.78	0.36	0.41	0.10
Barcelona	3.01	6.19	2.67	5.20
Barquisimeto	2.26	2.35	7.46	5.33
Maracaibo	3.30	8.88	11.72	25.02
Cuidad Bolivar	1.36	3.58	1.79	4.38
Cumana	3.07	7.55	0.58	1.33
Puerto Cabello	6.36	2.78	8.49	1.68
Guarenas	0.27	0.13	0.19	0.14
Guatire	-	-	0.04	0.03
San Cristobal	3.27	10.79	2.11	5.62
Merida	0.11	0.28	1.18	2.36
Maturin	2.73	9.01	0.64	1.97
Caracas	27.63	12.75	12.10	7.24
	62.76	65.67	54.78	61.34
Others	37.24	34.33	45.22	38.66
Total	100.00	100.00	100.00	100.00

8,428.3 Tons	8,247.9 Tons
2,023,250 Ton Km	2,273,320 Ton Km

APPENDIX C

Capital-Output Ratios for Transportation in Venezuela

In this appendix, we take the estimates available for gross capital investment in the Venezuelan transport industry--rights-of-way, vehicles, maintenance and repair facilities, storage terminals, docks, and the like--for a series of years from 1955. The gross capital formation estimates like those of the stock of capital investment are taken from working papers made available by the staff of the national income division of the Banco Central de Venezuela.   Its cooperation at every stage of this analysis must be acknowledged.

It will be observed that in general the average capital-output ratio fell throughout the period.   That is to say, gross capital invested in the transport sector tended to rise faster than did the gross domestic product originating in that sector.   By contrast, though more variable by far, the marginal capital-output ratio tended toward an increase.   This would seem to imply that the additions to the capital stock--of which the highway under study was an important element--were increasingly more productive.

TABLE C-I
Transport as a Per Cent of GDP: Venezuela

1950	5.08
1955	4.50
1956	4.04
1957	3.47
1958	3.65
1959	3.70
1960	3.23
1961	3.37

TABLE C-II
Transport Output-Capital Ratios: Venezuela

	(1) Estimated Gross Capital in Transport (000,000 Bs)	(2) Gross Capital Formation in Transport (000,000 Bs)	(3) Gross Domestic Product Originating in Transport (000,000 Bs)	(4) Average Output-Capital Ratio 3 1	(5) Marginal Output-Capital Ratio 3 2
1961	8,120	722	897	0.1104	1.2423
1960	7,820	775	911	0.1165	1.1754
1959	7,340	1,066	965	0.1315	0.9052
1958	5,560	410	882	0.1586	2.1512
1957	5,150	398	828	0.1608	2.0804
1956	4,750	1,058	820	0.1726	0.7750
1955	3,690	925	870	0.2358	0.9405

63

CHART 3

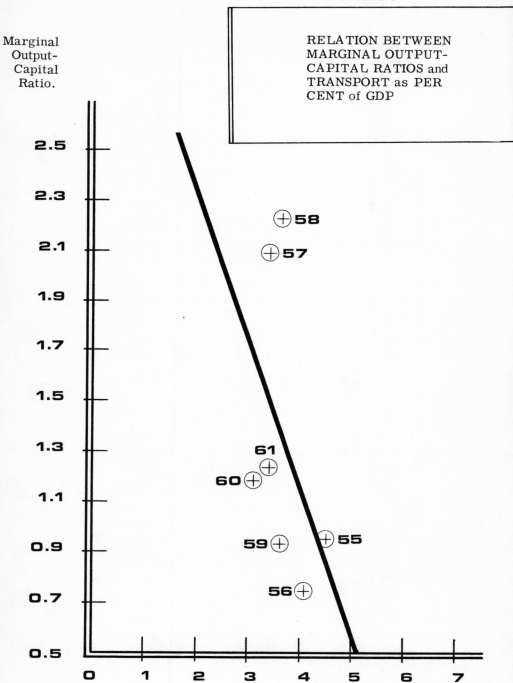

Marginal
Output-
Capital
Ratio.

RELATION BETWEEN
MARGINAL OUTPUT-
CAPITAL RATIOS and
TRANSPORT as PER
CENT of GDP

Transport as Per Cent of GDP

APPENDIX D

Thoughts on Highway Maintenance in Venezuela

One of the vexing problems in the economic analysis of highway benefits is that cost element is involved in maintenance. In
its study of the highway investment policy of the Ministry of
Public Works of Venezuela, the World Bank thought it necessary to criticize severely the lack of adequate maintenance.
Leaving aside whether these criticisms are justified by the
facts, there is a theoretical issue[22] involved that deserves
airing.

From one viewpoint, one may speak of the total user cost of
a highway. This total user cost is the sum of the amortized
capital cost and the maintenance necessary to preserve the productive value until the end of the economic life of the facility.
In turn, the maintenance cost may be thought of as the cost of
insuring a continued flow of traffic at the design or expected
level. Maintenance is thus a positive monotonic function of
traffic. It may, of course, decline per vehicle unit as total
traffic increases.

At any moment of time, highway maintenance can be substituted
for vehicle operating costs. If a road is maintained at a high
standard, the capital input for each unit of transport capacity
(vehicle depreciation, for example) can be reduced as vehicle
life increases. But if, by contrast, a road is maintained at
less than the standard calls for, capital input per transport unit
must increase.

With limited resources for highway maintenance, a nation may
allocate maintenance by actual traffic rather than by design
standard. This appears to be the policy of the Ministry of Public Works. In this context, a failure to maintain at the design
standard is not necessarily a waste of resources. There may,
however, have been a waste implicit in the construction design
standard itself.

Thus, if an overdesigned highway is in fact a waste of resources
in the first instance--by which we mean that its annualized total
costs are greater than any conceivable benefit that can be derived from the use of the highway--then maintenance at the design standard is simply a compounding of this waste.

More to the point in the Venezuelan case, where few examples
of low benefit exist, is the decision to take care of those highways where need rather than design indicates the action to be
taken. A rational procedure appears to be one which lowers
user costs, maintenance being its adjustable element, toward
the benefit represented by the actual traffic.

Traffic is itself a variable which multiplied by the necessary
value term yields an estimate of the contribution of the highway to the gross domestic product. The net benefit or contribution of the highway to the domestic product is obtained by
subtracting the maintenance and other elements of the user costs.
That level of maintenance which assures a maximum level of
net benefit from each highway is that which would appear to be
indicated.

In a more general sense, maintenance may be regarded as
being indifferent with new construction or vehicle purchase.
Any decision to have less of one means at given levels of transport "output" more of the other. Without knowing the price
mechanism at work, the equilibrium is not apparent.

APPENDIX E

Comments on a Classification of Effects of Transport
Facilities in Economic Development

There is an apparent need for a general classification of economic development effects which may be traced to highway investments. The following outline was worked out in the Transport Research Program of the Brookings Institution as a means
of assisting scholars and researchers in the field. It is in part
based upon some fruitful suggestions contained in a mimeographed
memorandum by Oglesby and Grant. This outline has influenced
the study of the Valencia-Tejerias autopista and guided the re-
searcher in his search for effects.

I. Consequences to transport facility users

    A. Market Consequences

        1. changes in vehicle operating costs
        2. changes in time costs to commercial vehicles
        3. changes in volume and direction of freight movements
        4. changes in volume and direction of passenger move-
           ments
        5. changes in the financial position of transport firms
        6. changes in the types of vehicle used (size, character,
           etc.)
        7. changes in the type of product transported
        8. changes in inventory costs, warehousing and handling
           procedures
        9. changes in the reliability of scheduled movements
     10. changes in the prices of commodities transported

    B. Extramarket Consequences

        1. Money as an arbitrary measure of consequence
           a. tourism
           b. time costs of noncommercial travel
           c. improvements in safety

        2. Impossible to assign money value
           a. parks, recreational facilities
           b. acculturation and integration of social
             classes, races, migrant groups

  c. slums (urban and rural)
  d. political unification together with improved provision
  e. improvement of communications channels and effect on market information

II. Consequences to other than transport facility users in the path and the impacted area of the transport facility

 A. Market Consequences

  1. cost changes in the provision of public services
  2. changes in agricultural land values or in the value/price of crops and natural resources
  3. changes in commercial and industrial land values
  4. changes in urban land usage patterns

 B. Extramarket Consequences

  1. over-all impact of transport facility on the economic, social, and political well-being and stability of a region/nation
  2. sequent occupance-intensive/extensive, positive/negative
  3. emergence of entrepreneurial ability

III. Consequences to region and/or nation (users and nonusers) including and beyond impacted area

 A. Market Consequences

  1. changes in income (levels, distribution, sources-- as between regions, classes, and industries)
  2. changes in employment
  3. changes in investment
  4. changes in public finance (tax sources, differential revenue patterns)
  5. changes in export/import, balance of trade, terms of trade, etc.
  6. spread of money economy

B.   Extramarket Consequences

1.   population changes--rates of increase, distribution, in-and-out migration
2.   relative "importance" of region (or city or nation or industry)
3.   means of determining criteria for private and/or public investment
4.   changes in nature and fact of political barriers (problems of common markets, regional integration, etc.)
5.   changes in the internal and external network of transport facilities
6.   development of social and political infrastructure

This is a much-modified scheme based on that originally developed by Oglesby and Grant.

Notes to Chapter 2

[1] Major portions were completed in 1958. Entire highway--Valencia to Tejerias--was not open until 1961. However, the section Tejerias-Caracas now finished "completes"the highway.

[2] See Appendix B for Origin-Destination Survey. Information on Railway traffic is from various Memoria, Banco Central de Venezuela.

[3] International Bank for Reconstruction and Development, The Economic Development of Venezuela,(Baltimore, 1961).

[4] R. M. Soberman, The Cost of Road Transportation in Venezuela, Corporacion Venezolana de Guayana, (Caracas: 1963), pp. 29-42.

[5] C. O. Meiberg, "An Economic Analysis of Highway Services", Quarterly Journal of Economics, November, 1963, pp. 648-656.

[6] Cordon counts by the Ministerio de Obras Publicas.

[7] Informe Economico Sobre Un Plan Ferroviario Nacional Comision Economica Ferroviaria Nacional, (Caracas: 1960).

[8] Memoria, Banco Central de Venezuela, 1961.

[9] Calculation of Breakeven Traffic for Railroad

$$X = \frac{I(C_f - 1/3\ C_c) + G_{ff} - G_{fe}}{ge - gf}$$

C_f = construction cost per km of railway, Bs 9,690,000
C_c = construction cost per km of highway, Bs 9,690,000
I = interest rate 0.08
G_{ff} = total operating cost - railway/km, Bs 6,760,000
G_{fe} = total operating cost - highway/km, Bs 1,690,000
gf = unit cost per ton km, railway, Bs 0.06
ge = unit cost per ton km, highway, Bs 0.12
x = ton kms = 93,113,000

[10] See Appendix B.

[11]Sergio Sanchez in 1961 attempted an evaluation of time savings resulting from the provision of a higher standard highway for the route, Caracas-Puerto Ordaz. Because some of this route to the Guayana lies in the Aragua Valley and passes in general through terrain similar to it, these estimates which run from a minimum of Bs 3 per hour for an automobile to a maximum of Bs 14 an hour for trucks, are used. See memo from Sergio Sanchez Naranjo to Roberto Alamo Blanco, dated 11 May 1961, Corporacion Venezolana de Guayana.

[12]The weights take into account the breakdown between organized trucking companies and individual truckers and the amount of freight each type of freight mover carried. Distance is also taken into account since per kilometer rates are not constant.

[13]The year 1959 is used because of availability of data. See Appendix B.

[14]Pipeline construction, maintenance and transport costs are so low compared with other forms of transport that the analyst is tempted to pass over the fact that this low cost may mask the relatively low secondary development productivity of such a transport investment. Compare this kind of investment with that in railways designed in the first instance to carry grains and cattle out of the Argentine pampa.

[15]Between the years 1954 and 1962, for example, the net export income from petroleum sector exports ranged between $900 million and $2 billion. This is net of sector imports and remittances as well as capital investments. The gross figures range upward of $1 billion more.

[16]This advantage, of course, arises from the saving both in time and in education outlay. Not all observers regard the in-migration as a net advantage, however. It should be noted that there has been a rapid expansion of technical education since 1952 and that by 1961-62, for example, there was an enrollment of 51,000 in technical schools.

[17]Cf. C. J. Stokes, "A Theory of Slums," Land Economics, August, 1962, pp. 187-197.

[18]Essentially, of course, this is a spelling out in a spatial context of the Schumpeterian argument of the effects of innovation and the entrepreneur. It also resembles Hicks' explanation of how growth occurs in cities. See J. R. Hicks, Essays on World Economics, Oxford, 1959. Especially pp. 162-74.

[19]An interesting pioneer attempt to measure the flow of funds in the Venezuelan economy was made by Harlow Osborne. See his study in Memoria, Banco Central de Venezuela, 1962. A significant part of his findings is that most of the flow of funds was generated by small entrepreneurs and the professional classes.

[20]Cf. Gunnar Myrdal, Rich Lands and Poor, New York, 1957, esp. Part One.

[21]See Appendix C for a short spelling out of the relation between capital-output ratios, gross domestic product, and the output of the transport industry in Venezuela in the 1950's.

[22]This appendix benefits from conversations in Lima, Peru, with Albert Hirschman, but it must not be taken to represent his viewpoint of the matter.

CHAPTER **3** THE FREIGHT
TRANSPORT
SYSTEM OF
COLOMBIA

THE FREIGHT TRANSPORT SYSTEM OF COLOMBIA

The freight transport system of Colombia is a complex one, far more complex than that which might be expected of a nation of its size and at its stage of economic development. This very complexity, however, provides a basis for the analysis of the assumed competitive relationship between various transport modes in developing countries.

In this chapter, the dimensions of the Colombian transport system are first considered, with the emphasis entirely upon freight rather than passenger movement. These dimensions both physical and economic are then analyzed in two ways. The Colombian transport system is studied as a set of transport subsystems, each subsystem being a different mode of transport. Then, by contrast, the basic transport system is broken down into area subsystems, each of which constitutes the complex of transport modes which each growth area had developed to solve its problem of transporting the goods it sells and buys. Thus, we are enabled to see the transport system not only as an interrelationship of "competing" modes--the way in which many observers of Colombian economic development have been wont to see the matter--but also as the result of the attempts of each key center in the nation to solve the transport problem facing it.

Though a number of excellent studies of the Colombian transport system have been published in recent years, many the results of original research, the present article does not depend upon any of these.[1] Rather, it was made possible by a careful origin and destination study done for the year 1959 by the Chilean economist, Norman Gillmore.[2]

This O & D study, combined with data obtained from Avianca--Colombia's largest air transportation company--as well as from the Departmento Administrativo de Planeacion, the Departmento Administrativo Nacional de Estadisticas, and the Ministerio de Obras Publicas, permits a complete assessment of the Colombian transport system in terms of the movement of freight for year 1959.

Begun as a case study of the impact of air cargo movement upon the economic development of Colombia sponsored by the Brookings Institution, this chapter is the result of an attempt to determine the relative importance of any one mode of transport. The methods worked out are presented in the expectation that they will aid

MAP 4

COLOMBIA

in avoiding arid arguments over investment priorities in transport planning on the one hand[3] and, on the other, will illustrate
how important a knowledge of the essential geographical problems of each region and nation are to an understanding of the
existing transport complex.

AN OVERVIEW

A better picture of the essence of the Colombian freight transport system can be gained with the aid of a series of maps.   The
first is a physical map (Map 4) indicating the nature of the terrain, the location of the principal natural highways, and the
principal cities.   A second map presents the existing (1959)
transport system composed of highways, railways, air cargo
lines, river transport, intracoastal waterways, and oil pipelines (Map 5).   Standing out on this second map are the key
transport centers along with the lesser centers of the nation.
Even more clear is the fact that, of all the different modes of
transport, only one, air cargo lines, provides a connection to
all parts of Colombia.   Each of the other modes tends to be part
of subsystems focused in turn upon each of the major growth centers.   It is this fact that has escaped many an observer of Colombian economic development.   And it is this fact which suggests
that it will be necessary to study the transport subsystems of
Colombia from two quite different standpoints, the one which dis-
tinguishes the different transport modes and the other which sep-
arates the transport subsystem developed for each city from
every other city-oriented transport subsystem.

Before we begin our analysis of the two possible approaches to a
study of Colombian transport subsystems it will be useful to have
some idea of the economic dimensions of the over-all system.   In
this way, we can at once see both the impressive size of the system and why the statistical relation among the various modes has
caused problems.

In 1959, the transport system carried 30.1 million (metric) tons
and 6.8 billion ton kilometers of freight (Tables I and II).   The
magnitudes and relationships shown in the tables indicate the extent to which the nation is dependent upon transport and, in fact,
upon each individual mode of transport.   That dependence, however, in the total sense, is not unduly heavy when compared with
that of other nations. [4]   These tables, moreover, do not give a

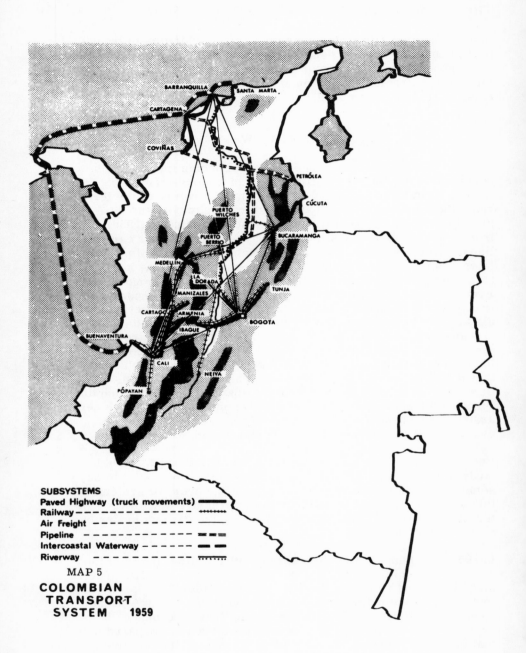

SUBSYSTEMS

Paved Highway (truck movements)	▬▬▬
Railway	‒‒‒‒‒‒‒ +++++++
Air Freight	‒‒‒‒‒‒‒‒‒‒
Pipeline	‒‒‒‒‒‒‒‒ ▬▬ ▬▬
Intercoastal Waterway	‒ ‒ ‒ ‒ ‒
Riverway	‒‒‒‒‒‒‒‒ ∷∷∷∷∷

MAP 5

COLOMBIAN
TRANSPORT
SYSTEM   1959

TABLE I

Freight Movement, Colombia, 1959, by Type of Product

Type of Product	Thousands of Tons	Per Cent of Total	Thousands of Tons	Per Cent of Total
Manufactured Goods	10.8	35.9	2.06	30.3
Petroleum (crude & refined)	8.5	28.2	2.89	42.4
Agricultural Produce	4.8	15.9	0.74	10.9
Mineral Products	3.8	12.6	0.71	10.4
Forestry Products	1.3	4.3	0.20	2.9
Animals	0.9	3.0	0.21	3.1

TABLE II
Freight Movement, Colombia, 1959, by Transport Mode

Transport Mode	Thou-sands of Tons *Millions tons*	Per Cent of Total	Thou-sands of Tons-Km *billions Moore*	Per Cent of Total
Highway Transport	17.2	57.0	2.46	35.9
Pipelines	8.5	28.1	2.89	42.2
Railways	2.7	8.9	.62	9.1
Riverways	1.4	4.6	.60	8.8
Intracoastal Waterways	.3	1.0	.24	3.5
Air Cargo	.1	0.3	.05	0.7

particularly accurate picture of the relative importance of the several individual modes to the nation, but how does one make a "for the want of a nail a battle is lost" analysis? Some progress can be made by separating out the noncompetitive elements and by determining the extent of complementarity among the different transport modes.

There is little question that highway transport and the pipelines share the bulk of the freight movement. Very clearly, however, there is no sense in which highway transport is competitive with pipeline transport since the shipper of crude oil and its many distillates could not choose highway transport. [5] Nor are pipelines available for the transport of any other product. However, the same cannot be said of the remaining modes of transport, and the temptation is to conclude, as in fact Norman Gillmore did, [6] that the relative share of the gross freight movement represents the relative strength of the competing mode of transport. In that light, there is little point to any intensive concentration upon the roles of the intercoastal waterways or the air cargo lines. Yet the fact of the high degree of connectivity revealed by the map of the air cargo lines puts this conclusion into doubt.

Because of its obvious noncompeting nature, we can eliminate the movement of crude and refined petroleum by pipeline from our analysis. And we can also reduce the gross freight movement picture to more meaningful dimensions by distinguishing between that freight which moves to and from within the economic zone of each growth area to the key city and that which moves between major economic regions.

Nonlocal freight movement is a more useful point of departure for analysis because it places the relative importance of particular transport modes into a context which reduces the importance of the fact that each economic region tends to have a unique transport subsystem. It is in these terms that we are able to compare the modal transport subsystems.

The degree of complementarity among the various modes of transport can be examined from two points of view. We can, on the one hand, look carefully at the maps to determine how goods moving from any one center to another or out of the country must travel. For example, from the map it is clear that goods traveling by land from Bogota to the Pacific Ocean port of Buenaven-

tura cannot travel all the way by rail; in fact, the journey is
broken between Ibague and Armenia. Likewise, goods pro-
ceeding upstream from Barranquilla to Bogota must be trans-
ferred to rail at Puerto Salgar (La Dorada). By the same token,
Puerto Berrio serves as the point of transshipment for Medellin
between the river and the Pacific Railway. In short, there are
relatively few land routes in the nation which do not require some
combination of transport modes. On the other hand, as will be
seen in the analysis of the city-oriented transport subsystems,
the degree of complementarity can be looked at in terms of the
transport task facing each city.

Each subsystem has its own characteristics, but the outstanding
characteristic of all but the air cargo system is the fragmented
nature of the subsystem network. In fact, the maps would cause
a careful observer to have doubts whether it is proper to speak,
for example, of a national rail system. Another characteristic
of each subsystem is that each seems to be designed to provide
a means of access from a key city to a frontier point, an ocean
port, or a border entrepot.

It is useful to compare the subsystems in terms of their connectivity using the criteria outlined by Kansky. [7] Indicators shown
in Table III have been developed. The alpha coefficient indicates
the degree of connectivity. It is a cyclomatic number or an arith-
metical comparison between the individual elements of the system
and the diameter. Essentially, it is a ratio between the number of
edges (routes), vertices (nodes), and the number of subgraphs
(isolated networks). The coefficient beta is somewhat simpler
and relates routes to nodes. The theta coefficient is a ratio of
the subsystem viewed as total traffic flow to the number of vertices. The theta coefficient measures the intensity of use of each
subsystem for all the traffic moving over it. Theta$_2$ measures
the intensity for all traffic moving between five key centers,
and theta$_3$ measures the intensity for all manufactured goods
traffic between five key cities.

For the alpha coefficient, air cargo, not surprisingly, has the
highest value. The highway system has a small positive value.
All other values are zero. In effect, this coefficient demonstrates
the lack of connectivity of the major subsystems. The beta coefficient which tends to measure the complexity of the system
assigns highest value to the highway network, but the range of
difference between networks is no greater than 2-1/2 to 1. The

TABLE III
Comparisons of Connectivity

	Alpha	Beta	$Theta_1$	$Theta_2$	$Theta_3$
Air Cargo System	.7	.50	22.3	7.9	6.5
Rail	0	.77	73.6	19.4	36.0
Road	.077	1.08	372.6	69.4	35.7
River	0	.75	117.9	88.2	110.8
Ocean-intracoastal	0	.43	40.3	2.6	1.5

Alpha = Degree, Beta = Complexity, $Theta_1$ = Intensity of use (all traffic), $Theta_2$ = Intensity of use (all five city traffic), $Theta_3$ = Intensity of use (all five city manufacturing traffic).

83

theta coefficient focuses upon particular aspects of the utilization of the subsystems. Despite the high degree of connectivity
of the air cargo system the highway system is most intensively
used, but for movement between five key centers the river
system is most intensively used.

These coefficients permit us to assess the relative utility of each
mode. However, though they tell us something about potential
efficiency as well as relative efficiency of use, they do not permit us to say which subsystem is best for any one purpose.

More useful, then, is an indicator of the degree of dependence
each major center has with respect to any one mode (Table IV).
This is presented in terms of the percentage of all and of manufactured goods traffic carried by each mode, for routes running
to and from each major center. The figures refer only to nonlocal traffic. From this table we can see that in 1959 air cargo
movements, for example, were significantly more important for
particular cities than the over-all statistics would indicate. Thus,
some 55% of all manufactured goods in and out of Bogota was
moved by air. By contrast, highway cargo movements were
large in relative proportion only for Bogota and Medellin. In
addition, we can say that Cali depended heavily upon rail traffic
and Bucaramanga and Baranquilla were just as heavily dependent
upon river traffic. A different structure of dependency, in fact,
emerges for each of the five major centers in the nation.

Only as we focus our attention upon the key cities of Colombia
do we come to see the nub of the "for the want of a nail the battle
was lost" problem. We really can't say very much about the relative importance of any one transport mode in Colombia until we
know how important it is for each route and for key centers. In
this light, it is obvious that little if any competition between transport modes exists and that, in fact, complementarity among modes
is the basic interrelationship. The shares of total traffic carried
reflect the nature of the economic development of each transport
mode.

SUBSYSTEMS BY MODE

There are at least six transport subsystems if we look at them in
terms of the mode of transport. For each subsystem a map is
presented indicating its general physical outline (Maps 6-11). On

TABLE IV
Degree of Dependency (In Percentages)

	Air		River		Rail		Ocean		Road	
	All	Mfr.	All	Mfr.	All	Mfr.	All	Mfr.	All	Mfr.
Bogota	24.5	55.5	3.4	3.4	15.9	16.6	-	-	56.3	24.5
Medellin	3.9	6.7	33.0	48.8	24.7	25.7	2.6	0.0	35.8	18.8
Cali	6.5	3.8	-	-	64.5	66.0	20.1	23.0	8.9	7.2
Barranquilla	17.8	7.9	63.1	69.5	-	-	19.1	22.6	-	-
Bucaramanga	1.2	3.9	66.3	69.5	23.5	29.6	-	-	1.0	-

each map is the amount of nonlocal cargo movement in and out
of each of the major centers in the nation, together with a table
indicating freight movement along important routes. Freight
movement in and out of each center is also indicated so that we
can see in rough terms the balance of local trade for each major center. [8]

The air cargo subsystem (Map 6) is the complex of air lines
offering cargo service. Airports serve every major center and
most of the smaller cities throughout the country including the
llanos and the jungle country south and east of the Andes. This
subsystem had been the fastest growing transport mode until the
middle 1950's when the growth ceased and the amount of cargo
moved by air began to decline.

A quarter of all traffic moves on the Bogota-Barranquilla route,
and the relative decline in all traffic moving along this route may
help in large measure to explain what has been happening to internal air cargo shipments. It is possible, too, that the opening
of the large international airport at El Dorado outside of Bogota
which sharply reduced the previous dependence on Barranquilla for
overseas air cargo handling may be a further explanation. The
expansion of the Cali airport to international jet dimensions may
continue the decline. This suggests that the air cargo decline is
more a matter of definition than reality. That is to say, much of
the movement along the one key route which generated a quarter
of all freight traffic had actually been export-import trade rather
than domestic goods shipments. Though it is not possible with
the current figures to rebuild the data in terms of domestic movement alone, it is at least useful to have in mind these cautionary
remarks. [9]

The most complete and perhaps the least intensively used, the
air cargo subsystem is also the most flexible. Enough has been
said to indicate that its relative importance cannot be judged
from comparison of absolute tonnage figures alone. On the other
hand, there is little basis for speculation about the development
role of air cargo, however interesting that speculation might be.

The intercoastal subsystem (Map 7) is so completely dependent
upon the availability of the Panama Canal that it would be a mis-
take not to underline its importance. Without this fact, it would
be difficult to explain the unique development of a cabotage system for a nation whose mobility index is so low. [10]

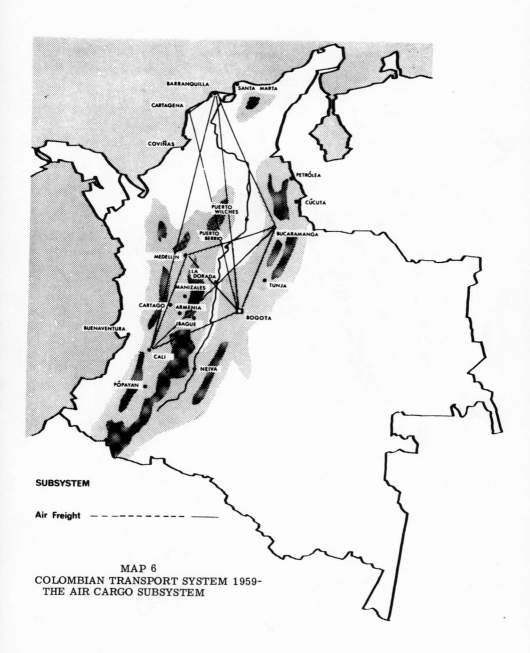

SUBSYSTEM

Air Freight — — — — — — — — — — —

MAP 6
COLOMBIAN TRANSPORT SYSTEM 1959-
THE AIR CARGO SUBSYSTEM

87

SUBSYSTEM

Intercoastal Waterway – – – – – ▬ ▬

MAP 7
COLOMBIAN TRANSPORT SYSTEM 1959–
THE INTERCOASTAL SUBSYSTEM

In effect there is but one route, that extending from Santa Marta on the northeast coast to Buenaventura on the central Pacific coast, though the routing does continue for minor shipments as far as Tumaco. As indicated by the map, some cargo does reach Medellin via the intercoastal subsystem, transshipped either by rail from Buenaventura or by riverboat and rail from Barranquilla. The most intensive use of the basic route occurs between Cartagena and Cali (Buenaventura) with most of the traffic moving from the Atlantic ports to the Pacific rather than vice versa.

The Magdalena River steamboat has always been symbolic of the Colombian transport system. But as the 1959 figures demonstrate, the river subsystem (Map 8) continues to be very intensively used for some of the nation's most important routes, Bogota to Barranquilla, Barranquilla to Medellin, and Barranquilla to Bucaramanga.

Barranquilla receives more tonnage than it ships, a good share of it coming from Santander Department, indicating the importance of petroleum products in the total river cargo consist. Both Bogota and Medellin receive significantly more than they ship by riverboat. In fact, Bogota originates very little river traffic. These observations would imply that, as might be expected, the riverboats are used for the transport of raw materials, generally bulk goods.

Neither the intracoastal waterway subsystem nor the river subsystem show any significant postwar changes in relative importance. This is largely traceable to the fact that for the routes they serve and the cargo carried there is little if any alternative.

The rail subsystem (Map 9), as noted previously, was in 1959 largely two or three separate rail networks. During 1959, connection was made between the Pacific Railway at Puerto Berrio and The Gran Sabana network at La Dorada, making possible for the first time all-rail freight service from a seaport to the nation's capital. This was so circuitous a routing, however, that it was unlikely to play a significant role in freight movement. Rather this link was later used as a part of the Atlantic Railway which was extended from Puerto Berrio to Santa Marta--but not Barranquilla--on the Atlantic Coast in 1961. This

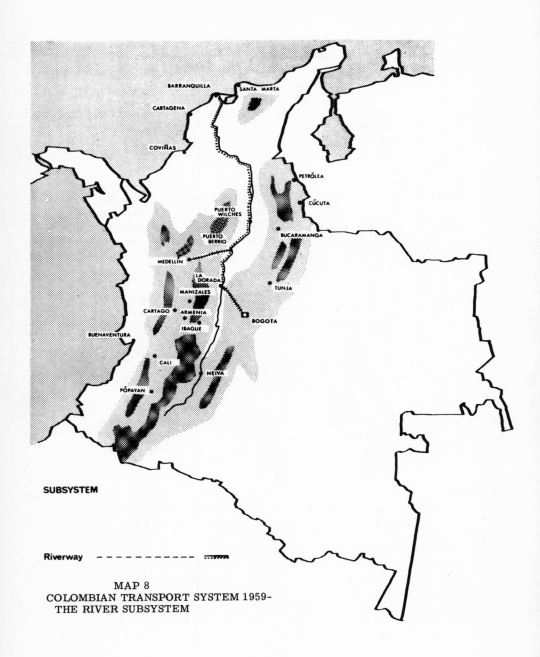

SUBSYSTEM

Riverway – – – – – – – – – – –

MAP 8
COLOMBIAN TRANSPORT SYSTEM 1959-
THE RIVER SUBSYSTEM

SUBSYSTEM

Railway ----------------- +++++++

MAP 9
COLOMBIAN TRANSPORT SYSTEM 1959-
THE RAIL SUBSYSTEM

91

became the second all-rail connection between Bogota and a seaport.

The total tonnage handled by rail was, nonetheless, quite large, both in relative terms--that is, as a share of the national freight waybill--and in comparison with other developing nations with more complete rail systems having much higher connectivity. [11] If we add that the share of traffic carried by rail was not shifting very much during the postwar period, it follows that the structure of transport modes was not being varied by the increased demands put upon them by the fast rising gross domestic product. [12]

The Cali-Bogota, the Cali-Manizales, and the Cali-Medellin routes were the important ones in Colombia in 1959, with Cali being a net shipper in tonnage terms. Manizales, too, the center of the coffee region, was a net shipper. All other major rail points were net receivers of freight.

The paved highway network (Map 10) is effectively the subsystem of highway freight service though the truck is every bit as flexible a vehicle as an airplane. But, as with rail, there is neither a single road system radiating from the nation's capital as is the case in so many developing nations nor any integrated road system from any other point. Rather there are road networks largely regionalized.

In contrast with rail and with river traffic, Bogota is a major shipping point for truck freight movements. The same is true of Medellín and Bucaramanga. The very heavy movement into Cucuta suggests the magnitude of the Venezuelan export trade, a good share of which is contraband. [13] The movements in and out of Barranquilla are entirely local, though the completion and partial paving of the Medellin-Cartagena-Barranquilla road ("Western Trunk Road") may have changed this picture during the early 1960's.

The heavy net truck movement into Cali suggests both the local character of the traffic and the dependence of Cali industry upon raw materials obtained within its hinterland. Interdepartmental routes, as shown, generally do not support heavy traffic. Most of the Bogota-Cali traffic, the busiest long route, was concrete and other industrial mineral raw materials.

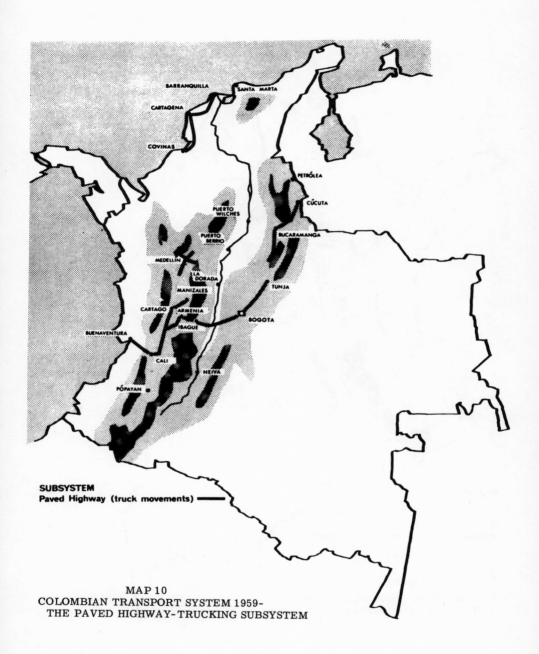

SUBSYSTEM
Paved Highway (truck movements) ———

MAP 10
COLOMBIAN TRANSPORT SYSTEM 1959-
THE PAVED HIGHWAY-TRUCKING SUBSYSTEM

93

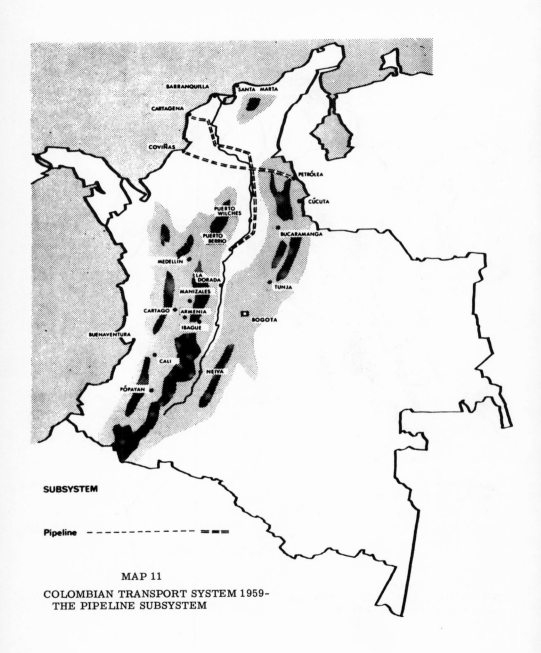

BARRANQUILLA

SANTA MARTA

CARTAGENA

COVIÑAS

PETRÓLEA

CÚCUTA

PUERTO
WILCHES

PUERTO
BERRIO

BUCARAMANGA

MEDELLIN

LA
DORADA

MANIZALES

TUNJA

CARTAGO   ARMENIA

BOGOTA

IBAGUE

BUENAVENTURA

CALI

NEIVA

PÓPAYAN

SUBSYSTEM

Pipeline ‑ ‑ ‑ ‑ ‑ ‑ ‑ ‑ ‑ ‑ ‑ ‑ ‑ ‑ ■ ■ ■

MAP 11

COLOMBIAN TRANSPORT SYSTEM 1959-
THE PIPELINE SUBSYSTEM

About the pipeline subsystem (Map 11), little need be said. Designed to carry crude and refined petroleum from the wells to river and ocean ports, they serve no major center.

These summary views of the modal subsystems reinforce the first impressions, namely, that Colombia does not have a set of competing transport modes and that, therefore, the concept of relative importance as determined by tonnage measures is not in general applicable there. Each mode has traffic characteristics which reflect the task assigned to it in view of the geographical barriers which separate the nation into so many distinct economic regions. In that sense, the modes are to a large degree complementary, so that reduction in adequacy of service on any one of them is likely to create a problem for the entire system and not to rebound to the advantage of a "competing" mode. To put the matter differently, the Colombian transport system viewed as a complex of modal subsystems is peculiarly a unity put together to solve the nation's transport problem.[14]

SUBSYSTEM BY MAJOR CITY

Five major cities tend to dominate the Colombian economy. How important these cities are relative to the nation can be seen in Table V; some 85% of the manufacturing value added, 78% of the gross domestic product, as well as about 60% of all nonlocal cargo is handled in through these cities. They, also, have a significant share of the manufacturing establishments, manufacturing employment, and installed horsepower, and are, in fact, the growth centers of the nation. Each, because of the geographical configuration, is the key city to a large economic area. These economic areas are essentially conterminous with the political subdivisions called departments. Their departments and their capitals are Cundinamarca (Bogota), Antioquia (Medellin), Valle (Cali), Atlantico (Barranquilla), and Santander (Bucaramanga). Valle and Antioquia lie on the western flank of the central range of the Andes. A mountain wall on the east rises above 22,000 feet. Valle and Antioquia are in turn separated by land at considerably lower altitudes. Cali is at about 3,000 feet and Medellin at about 5,000 feet. By the same token, Bogota is at 8,500 feet in the Gran Sabana, one of the richest temperate zone areas in the Andes, and Bucaramanga is at 3,500 feet. Far to the north on the Caribbean Coast is the department of Atlantico

TABLE V

Colombia: Five Major Cities, Relation Between Freight and Production and Employment Indicators
(ca. 1959)

	Bogota	Medellin	Cali	Barran-quilla	Bucara-manga	Total Per Cent 5 cities
Percentage of air cargo handled	25.3	10.2	6.7	13.8	1.8	67.8
Percentage of all nonlocal cargo	18.3	8.7	9.5	8.7	13.8	59.0
Percentage of nonlocal mfg. cargo	6.3	7.4	11.8	12.2	22.4	60.1
Percentage of gross domestic product	24.8	20.9	18.1	8.2	5.5	77.5
Percentage of mfg. value added	27.2	24.9	18.5	9.0	5.3	84.9
Percentage of mfg. employees	29.7	24.4	15.8	9.9	4.6	84.4
Percentage of mfg. wages	30.0	25.5	16.5	9.6	4.3	85.9
Percentage of installed horsepower	24.9	24.4	16.9	9.2	5.6	81.0
Annual growth rate	6.2	4.1	6.0	4.7	7.1	-

with Barranquilla at sea level, at the mouth of the Magdalena
River.

In general, the concentration of economic activities within each
department is such that it involves little error to treat the capital city and the department as one. Only in the case of Cali,
with its rich semitropical valley which has given rise to sat-
ellite city development and where the relationship between Cali
and Manizales in the department of Caldas is highly complementary, more care should be taken to distinguish between city
and hinterland, to determine the relative contribution of each.
Moreover, Cali is some 142 km from its Pacific Ocean port of
Buenaventura through which a major share of the nation's exports and imports move. Nonetheless, even in this case, it is
defensible to treat the region focusing upon Cali as if all activity
indeed did take place in Cali.

In Table VI, the distinction is made between all cargo movements
for each department and the movement of manufactured goods,
then for each of these categories is worked out the proportion
that is nonlocal, the proportion that moves between the key city
of the department and the other four key cities, and the modes
by which such movements took place in 1959. This enables us
to get a general picture of each city-oriented transport subsystem. Then follows a series of origin and destination tables for
each of the major cities, distinguishing between modes of transport. One set of such tables analyzes all cargo movements for
1959 and another analyzes manufacturing cargo only. In this
way, we can see how each city worked out the solution to its
basic transport problem and developed a system which in 1959
provided for the movement of the raw materials it used and the
products it produced.

If we analyze cargo shipments by major modes for each of the
five key transport centers in Colombia as is done in Table VI,
we can distinguish between the total cargo handled between the
city and all other shipping points within the nation, the nonlocal cargo, and the amount of cargo shipped between the five
key cities as well as the means by which this key city cargo
moved. This gives us still another measure of the degree of
dependence of each city upon different transport modes. But
it does something else as well: It enables us to see what had
to be transported and how each city solved its transport problem

TABLE VI

Analysis of Cargo Shipments by Major Modes, Five Departments, Colombia, 1959

Metric Tons (Add 000)	Atlantico (Barranquilla)		Antioquia (Medellin)	
	All Freight	Mfr. Cargo as a Per Cent of All Freight	All Freight	Mfr. Cargo as a Per Cent of All Freight
Total Freight	1,531.0	73.2	2,668.4	49.3
Nonlocal Freight	659.0	82.6	654.0	50.2
5-City Freight--Local	145.0	74.3	276.0	44.6
5-City Freight--By Mode				
Air	10.0	43.1	11.0	70.0
Cabotage	4.1	93.8	10.0	-
Rail	-	-	65.2	46.6
River	131.0	76.1	89.0	82.0
Truck	-	-	101.0	12.1

Metric Tons (Add 000)	Cundinamarca(Bogota)		Santander(Bucaramanga)		Valle (Cali)	
	All Freight	Mfr. Cargo as a Per Cent of All Freight	All Freight	Mfr. Cargo as a Per Cent of All Freight	All Freight	Mfr. Cargo as a Per Cent of All Freight
Total Freight	4,423.1	49.3	1,691.0	78.5	3,215.0	44.2
Nonlocal Freight	1,384.1	20.2	1,051.0	95.6	722.5	73.7
5-City Freight--Local	693.3	25.6	409.0	93.5	235.0	68.3
5-City Freight--By Mode						
Air	19.0	70.0	2.0	48.8	6.0	62.6
Cabotage	-	-	-	-	4.1	97.0
Rail	54.0	16.4	6.2	16.1	194.4	72.3
River	2.0	51.8	396.1	96.1	-	-
Truck	669.0	23.1	2.4	-	40.3	30.3

99

in 1959. The result is in effect the transport subsystem each
city had worked out, presumably, some years before 1959.
This information tends to confirm the hasty observations which
had been made from the map of Colombia; that is to say, each
city-oriented transport subsystem is the result of specific solutions in terms of what is shipped and the route chosen, given
the geography of the region, to the transport problems the city
faced. How much is moved by air, for example, from Bogota
to Barranquilla is the result of the cost, availability of alternative modes, and the nature of the goods to be transported.

In every case, the transport subsystem for each city is different
from that which the national totals might have led you to expect.
This follows from the relative modal share difference from city
to city. Thus, the national system while it is the sum of its
parts, is not really like any of its parts. Decisions made without regard to the distinctions between regional subsystems are
likely to be subject to error.

An origin and destination analysis gives an even clearer picture
of the city-oriented subsystems. Tables VII and VIII first give
traffic totals for all products in tonnage terms, then for manufactured goods shipments and for major categories of goods in
percentage terms. What emerges from this type of analysis is
the complexity of the solutions each city has worked out for its
transport problem.

When this approach is contrasted with that of modal subsystem,
we note that whereas it was not possible to detect a meaningful
breakdown between modes either for the year 1959 or for the
postwar period, when we turn to city-oriented subsystems, we
are able to see the role of each mode within a context that is
explanatory of the actual transport developments. The question
then is no longer how important the rail system is, but rather
how important it is to Cali and the Pacific Intermontane Region.
It is not whether air cargo movement is significant or not, but
how significant it is for Bogota and for movements of manufactured goods in and out of Bogota.

We don't attempt by this approach to assess the feasibility of
any further investments in any one modal subsystem. We take
the existing networks as given, attempt to see what their role
has been and why they are as they are. The advantage of this

approach is that it permits us to focus upon the geographical
aspects of Colombian transport that have been commented on
but seldom taken explicitly into consideration.

SUMMARY AND CONCLUSIONS

In the case of the Colombian transport system, we have observed
that it is not useful to think in terms of competition between modes.
The importance of this observation for an analysis of the impact
of transport investment of developing countries must be stressed.
There has been a persistent argument between supporters of one
or another mode with respect to which is most likely to produce
particular results in terms of additions to the gross national product or some other measure of benefit. In this case, and admitted-
ly this is a static view of the problem, it is clear that each of the
modes play a determinative role which must be seen in terms of
the cargo, the point of origin, and the route to be traveled. To
be sure the highly accidented geography of Colombia made necessary the selection of a wide variety of modes to solve the strik-
ingly different transport problems facing each of the key developing areas. Thus, the answer which emerges tentatively from this
analysis is that there is no clear superiority of one mode over
another in any national sense. For each route, each region, and
each major product category a different answer may be derived
and the transport system at any moment of time is the combination of these modes.

We are tempted to add, if this kind of analysis is at all applicable,
that the expenditure to construct the Atlantic Railway was unneces-
sary. The theory underlying the outlay was that there were only
fragments of a national rail system and that to integrate these
fragments to improve their ability to compete with other transport
modes, it was necessary to have a link at Puerto Berrio with the
Pacific Railway and at La Dorada with the system serving the
Gran Sabana along a line which would lead to an Atlantic port. [15]
The new line, however, must be seen in terms of what it does
to the city-oriented subsystems and to what extent it is necessary
to provide Bogota with an additional parallel route to the Atlantic.

The point of the chapter is that transport system evaluation requires a geographical as well as an economic frame of reference.
Against the background of geography, we can see the solutions

TABLE VII

Origin and Destination of Shipments: All Products, Five Major Cities, Colombia, 1959 (Percentages)

Origin

Destination

		Medellin	Cali	Bucaramanga	Barranquilla
I	Bogota				
	Rail	54.83	2.34	6.65	-
	River	-	-	0.24	13.55
	Ocean	-	-	-	-
	Truck	35.85	98.86	92.28	-
	Air	9.32	0.80	0.83	86.45

		Bogota	Cali	Bucaramanga	Barranquilla
II	Medellin				
	Rail	39.22	59.83	-	59.12
	River	0.13	-	72.94	10.41
	Ocean	-	-	-	-
	Truck	53.38	36.45	25.06	28.34
	Air	7.27	3.72	2.00	2.13

		Bogota	Medellin	Bucaramanga	Barranquilla
III	Cali				
	Rail	74.96	82.92	100	-
	River	-	-	-	-
	Ocean	-	-	-	-
	Truck	19.46	16.32	-	80.40
	Air	5.58	0.76	-	19.60

IV Barranquilla

	Bogota	Medellin	Bucaramanga	Cali
Rail	-	-	-	-
River	64.36	97.73	99.26	-
Ocean	-	0.27	-	82.20
Truck	-	-	0.74	-
Air	35.64	2.00	-	17.80

V Bucaramanga

	Bogota	Cali	Medellin	Barranquilla
Rail	71.02	-	-	-
River	-	-	99.39	99.70
Ocean	-	-	-	-
Truck	27.49	-	-	-
Air	1.49	-	0.61	.30

Sources: Various reports by Departamento Nacional de Estadistica, Colombia. N. Gillmore, La Futura Demanda de Transporte de Carga en Colombia, (Bogota; Departmento Administrativo de Planeacion, August, 1963), various tables.

103

TABLE VIII

Various Means of Transport--
Origin and Destination of Shipments of Manufactures by Colombia, 1959, Five Major Cities (Percentages)

Destination

Origin

I Bogota

	Cali	Medellin	Bucaramanga	Barranquilla
Rail	-	64.4	1.7	-
River	-	-	-	13.2
Ocean	-	-	-	-
Truck	-	-	97.5	-
Air	100	35.6	0.8	86.8

II Medellin

	Cali	Bogota	Bucaramanga	Barranquilla
Rail	15.39	87.35	-	-
River	-	0.37	98.09	96.63
Ocean	-	-	-	-
Truck	75.12	-	-	-
Air	9.48	12.27	1.90	3.36

III Cali

	Medellin	Bogota	Bucaramanga	Barranquilla
Rail	99.17	65.23	100.00	-
River	-	-	-	-
Ocean	-	-	-	-
Truck	-	29.04	-	92.25
Air	0.82	5.71	-	7.75

IV

Barranquilla	Medellin	Bogota	Bucaramanga	Cali
Rail	-	-	-	-
River	98.49	79.80	99.55	-
Ocean	0.33	-	-	90.14
Truck	-	-	-	-
Air	1.18	20.20	0.45	9.86

V

Bucaramanga	Bogota	Medellin	Barranquilla	Cali
Rail	88.49	-	-	-
River	-	99.36	99.69	-
Ocean	-	-	-	-
Truck	-	-	-	-
Air	11.51	0.64	0.31	-

evolved by each growth region to the problem of reaching the world beyond it.

The extent to which the resultant national system is integrated is not then a matter of whether there is connectivity within modal limits. Rather it is the effectiveness with which the over-all transport problem is solved. Integration in this sense, then, has to do with the way in which the modal fragments are put together for each route and each major freight category. Given the essentially static view of the problem in this chapter imposed by the limitations of the data, we cannot assess the degree of integration in this somewhat different sense. But we can hazard the observation that the 1959 transport map for Colombia is substantially more indicative of an effective solution than has been supposed.

Notes to Chapter 3

[1] Consejo Nacional de Politica Economica y Planeacion; Departamento Administrativo de Planeacion y Servicios Tecnico, Plan Cuatrienal de Inversiones Publicas Nacionales, 1961-1964; Department of State, United States of America: Highways, Special Report on Colombian Highway Transportation, Unpub. Report, May 4, 1962; Colombia, Ministerio de Obras Publicas: Memoria de Obras Publicas, 1961, Imprenta Nacional, 1962; Olap-Ingenieria, Tippetts-Abbett-McCarthy-Stratton: National Highway Program, Report to Ministerio de Obras Publicas, July, 1961; Parsons, Brinckerhoff, Quade & Douglas: Plan de Mejoramiento para los Transportes Nacionales, Ministerio de Obras Publicas, Bogota, Colombia, 1961, Ingles y Castellano; Robert R. Nathan Associates, Inc.: Programa de Desarrollo Economico del Valle de Magdalena y Norte de Colombia, Informe al Ministerio de Obras Publicas, preparacion dirigida por Lauchlin Currie, Bogota, 1960; Wolfgang Friedmann, Raymond Mikesell, George Kalmanoff, Public International Development Financing in Colombia, (New York: Department of International Legal Research of Columbia University and the Institute of International Studies and Overseas Administration of the University of Oregon, June, 1963), Chapter 4.

[2] Norman Gillmore: La Futura Demanda de Transporte de Carga En Colombia, (Bogota: Departmento Administrativo de Planeacion, August, 1963).

[3] See Eric E. Pollock's sage advice, "Transport Surveys and Forecasting," Paper contributed to the United Nations Conference on the Application of Science and Technology for the Benefit of the Less Developed Areas, October, 1962. See also, Note Sur Les Criteres Economiques de Choix des Operations du Secteur des Transports Susceptibles d'etre Inscrites au Ve Plan, (Paris: Commissariat General du Plan, November, 1963).

[4] About 3.5% of the Colombian labor force was employed in the transport sector. The sector itself contributed 6.4% of the net product. In rough terms, this indicated a relatively high productivity for the transport sector.

[5] He might, however, choose rail or river transport if it were available.

[6]Gillmore, op. cit. , p. 6, eliminates air cargo from consideration because of its small share and, therefore, its lack of importance.

[7]K. J. Kansky: Structure of Transportation Networks, Department of Geography Research Paper, No. 84 (Chicago: University of Chicago) 1963.

[8]In this case, total tonnage, not just nonlocal traffic.

[9]However, Appendix D of the Parsons-Brinckerhoff Colombia transport study reveals in some detail the changes by airport and by destination in the relative position of the key air cargo shipping points from 1953 to 1960.

[10]Wilfred Owen, on the basis of comparative data available to him in 1963, worked out an index relating per capita GNP to freight and passenger mobility. Colombia had a freight mobility index of 11. 3, about the median for the "immobile nations. " By comparison, that of Argentina was 63. 8 and of the United States, 189. 0. See Wilfred Owen, Strategy for Mobility (Washington, D. C. : Transport Research Program, The Brookings Institution, 1964) Chapter 1.

[11]See Robert T. Brown "The 'Railroad Decision' in Chile, " in Transport Investment and Economic Development, edited by Gary Fromm (Washington, D. C. : The Brookings Institution, 1965) pp. 242ff. Brown shows that the "integrated rail system" of Chile moves about four times as many ton kilometers as the Colombian rail system.

[12]Despite the rapid growth of the air cargo lines, far faster than the GNP, the actual tonnage carried on these lines was not large enough to change to essential relationships among all modes.

[13]See Posibilidades de Integracion de las Zonas Fronterizas Colombia-Venezuela, a Report for the Interamerican Development Bank, April, 1964. This includes the best available estimates of actual commerce across the border region.

[14]The transport problem is sometimes seen as that of the relative economic feasibility of particular modes. A problem is said to exist when, for example, rail revenues are insufficient to cover rail operating costs. That is not the sense in which we

view the transport problem.   Rather, here we are concerned
with the task of getting goods from one place to another against
the background of geographic obstacles.

[15]The selection of Santa Marta rather than Barranquilla
as the Atlantic Port is surprising, based in large part upon the
fact that a rail line already existed, running from Santa Marta
to Fundacion.   That there was no adequate dock development at
Santa Marta and that traditionally Barranquilla had served as the
major Atlantic port and, therefore, had the facilities for handling
such traffic, seems to have played little part in this decision.

CHAPTER **4** THE ECONOMIC
IMPACT OF THE
CARRETERA
MARGINAL DE LA
SELVA

THE ECONOMIC IMPACT OF THE
CARRETERA MARGINAL DE LA SELVA

One of the most dramatic highway proposals of recent times is
the South American plan to build an international road stretch-
ing 5,500 kilometers from the Colombian border with Venezuela
in the northeast to the city of Santa Cruz in south-central Bolivia.[1] Following in general the eastern side of the Andes through
the sabanas, jungles, foothills, and largely uninhabited and
even unsurveyed country in Colombia, Ecuador, Peru, and Bolivia, the Carretera Marginal de la Selva will, when completed,
open up vast areas of one of the world's last frontiers--the
Amazon-Orinoco plains in the heart of South America.

This chapter is a summary of research done to determine the
feasibility of the Carretera Marginal de la Selva. The study is
tentative in its conclusions largely because of the lack of adequate data, but it does outline the essential justification for the
highway which, as it turns out, is rather more convincing than
had been first assumed. It presents the reasons for our conclusion that the highway is an investment on the part of each nation
that will yield substantial benefits in excess of its costs. Some
of these benefits are direct and quantifiable in dollar terms.
These include the increase in farm production from areas that,
until this highway is complete, will have been negligible contri-
butors to national gross domestic products. They also include
the increase in the income from auxiliary activities as the entire
region develops. To this we might add the increase in foreign
earnings arising from a reduction in imports on one hand and an
increase in exports on the other. Finally, to the extent that the
Oriente becomes self-supporting, the central government's net
contribution may be reduced.[2]

The Carretera Marginal de la Selva will have a substantial impact upon the economies of the Andean countries. More than
1,590,000 people will be affected directly in Colombia, Ecuador,
Peru, and Bolivia, and many more indirectly. The completion
of the highway will bring into production 7,400,000 hectares representing $134,000,000 in value of annual farm production.

Other benefits are also direct but are not quantifiable in money
terms. They include the hectarage to be brought under cultivation, the total population to be settled in the areas being opened
up, the widening of production possibilities, and therefore the reduction of national dependence on a narrow range of crops. Direct
benefits are those which affect the zones of influence and are the

113

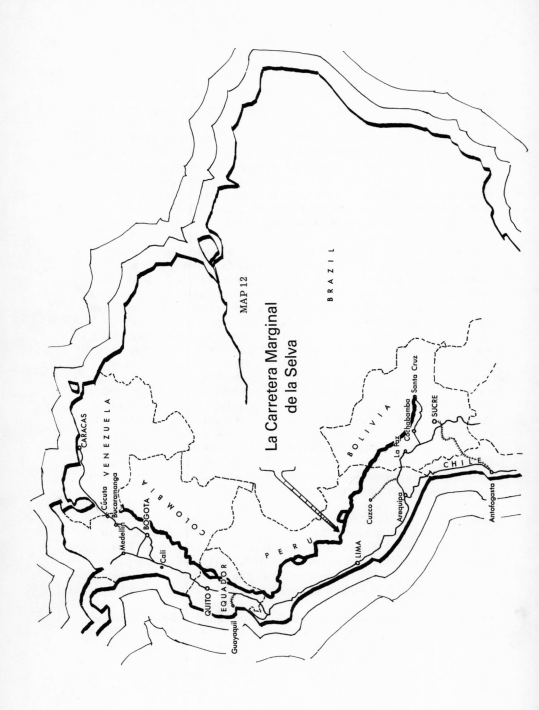

MAP 12

La Carretera Marginal
de la Selva

measure of the economic development to be expected in the Oriente as the Carretera Marginal is completed. For a summary of direct benefits and costs to each of the four nations, see Table I.

Still other benefits are indirect; that is to say, they affect the entire nation in a diffuse way. And some, indeed, represent potential gains for the family of Latin nations. Thus, it is possible to talk about gains from political integration within each nation as the interconnectivity of the transport system is greatly improved. Also, the differentials in development between regions within the nation will be reduced, permitting a more balanced growth and a reduction in the degree of concentration of economic activity in particular, favored areas. Looking beyond national frontiers, we can see advantages from the economic integration of these Andean nations (Colombia, Ecuador, Peru, and Bolivia) into a more effective common market. Moreover, the long-run influence of the highway upon the attainment of peace and understanding is one of the most significant benefits that may be derived from the project.

The costs of the highway are likewise direct and indirect. The direct costs are those we estimate to be the expense involved in the construction and maintenance of the highway and feeder roads as well as the provision of technical assistance, colonization aid, and other elements necessary to permit development of the expected zones of influence and adjacent areas. The indirect costs are the other uses to which the expected dollar amount of the highway complex outlay might be put.

INCREASED PRODUCTION

The most obvious direct benefits from the building of the Carretera Marginal are the expected increases in production. The most important economic activity in the zones being opened up is agriculture. In each of the countries we have estimated the production for each farm family at full development for each of the highway sections. In Table II this estimate is compared with our estimate of current production in these sections. The resultant increases, whether seen as dollar figures or as percentages, measure the benefit we anticipate from the highway.

TABLE I
Summary of Direct Benefits and Costs

	Colombia	Ecuador	Peru	Bolivia	Total
1. Annual value of farm production in full development (millions)	$ 35,118	13,960	36,409	13,084	$133,689
2. Regional product* at full development (millions)	$ 58,530	23,267	60,682	21,807	$164,286
3. Per capita product, zone of influence	$ 194	56	114	63	$ 103
4. Total population in area at full development (thousands)	302	412	530	348	1,593
5. Hectares made available(millions)	2,430	1,640	1,718	1,605	7,392
6. Cost of highway and other works (millions)	$113,100	81,300	227,800	71,800	$494,000

*Farm production assumed to be 60% of regional product.

116

TABLE II

Current and Expected Agricultural Production Per Farm Family in Zone
of Influence (In 1960 U.S. Dollars)

	Colombia	Ecuador	Peru	Bolivia
Range of gross farm product per farm family--individual sections at full development	$719-954	199-417	259-648	180-322
Estimated current product per farm family	$ 665	155	194	123
Range of expected increase in product per farm family	$ 54-289	44-262	65-259	57-179
Range of percentage increases	8.1-43.5	28.4-169.0	33.5-236.6	46.3-55.6
Expected percentage increase in GNP 1964-2004	155	107	200	60
Average annual rate of increase (per cent)	4.9	6.0	4.2	0.8

It should be noted that the actual range of income per farm family within each nation and indeed within each region is so great that it is not meaningful to compare these figures with national averages. The significant fact emerging from our analysis is that the range of percentage increases in Peru, Bolivia, and Ecuador includes sectors with rates of income growth exceeding those anticipated for the national. The Colombian situation is modified by the fact that substantial growth has already occurred in the llanos.

In every case, the anticipated level of per capita regional product represents a significant increase over current levels in the same, adjacent, or comparable regions in the nation. This may be taken to mean that farm families being formed in such areas will find it to their advantage to migrate.

POPULATION AND MIGRATION

An increase in the population of the zones of influence of the highway from a present estimated 161,000 to 1,592,000 may be anticipated by the time the full development of the land resources opened up has been achieved (Table III). Of the increase, some 962,000 represent the additional farm population. The migration to the area of the Carretera Marginal de la Selva will provide some significant relief from the population pressure in the Altiplano of Bolivia, where as many as one in every ten Bolivians may have new lands made available. For Peru, almost 500,000, representing 25 of every 1,000 Peruvians, will find new homes and economic opportunities during the period of development. The proportion of the Ecuadorian population for whom new farms will become available is essentially the same as that in Peru. In Colombia, where substantial migration into the llanos has already begun, it may be estimated that some 12 in every 1,000 will take advantage of the new farm lands made available. Thus, the Carretera Marginal de la Selva will represent an important element in resource planning. Combined with land reform and colonization, a more equitable and productive distribution of land will be achieved for the Andean nations.

HECTARAGE OPENED

The placing in cultivation of 600,000 hectares in the four countries

TABLE III

Expected Migration into Zone of Influence

	Colombia	Ecuador	Peru	Bolivia	Total
Population now in zone of influence	79,000	25,000	51,000	6,000	161,000
Population anticipated at full development	302,000	412,000	530,000	348,000	1,592,000
Farm migration into area	114,000	270,000	341,000	237,000	962,0C0

TABLE IV

Expected Increase in Available Croplands Resulting from Carretera Marginal de la Selva

	Colombia	Ecuador	Peru	Bolivia
Hectares in cultivation ca. 1960	3,472,800	1,590,000	1,995,100	835,300
Hectares in cultivation in zone of influence at full development	182,000	130,000	186,000	102,000
Per cent gross addition to current cultivable area	5.2	8.2	9.3	12.2

through which the highway passes is, of course, a significant
addition to current crop areas, ranging from a gross increment
of 5.2% in Colombia to one of 12.2% in Bolivia (Table IV).   This
direct benefit will permit a substantial increase in production,
not only in the regions affected, but in the nations taken all
together.   More important, perhaps, is the fact that this new
land will make possible a diversification of agricultural production and trade.   For Peru, for example, the Selva and Ceja de
la Montana provide the possibility of great increases in tropical
agriculture, both for export and domestic consumption, for a nation that has up to now specialized in temperate and subtropical
crops.   Similar opportunities exist in Bolivia.   In Ecuador, where
tea is being introduced in the Oriente, there is an indication of the
broadening base of potential exports.

The incorporation of the soil resources into the farm economy will
have effects domestically and internationally, quite possibly beyond the scope of current forecasts.   These possibilities are outlined in the following section.

INTERPRETING THE BENEFITS

When the benefit horizon is distant in time, as is the case for the
Carretera Marginal de la Selva, the spelling out of benefits also
attempts to account for the dynamic changes likely to occur in the
zone of influence, as well as in each of the nations.   The peculi-
arities of tropical agriculture play an important role in any estimates of benefits.   The Carretera Marginal de la Selva opens to
penetration the largest undeveloped tropical areas in the world,
the drainage areas of the Orinoco and Amazon systems.   Agrono-
mists are searching for crops, techniques, and land use patterns
which will be especially adaptable to the conditions of these regions.

While it is true that some of the soils of this region are currently
regarded as poor, there may be reason to anticipate a change in
this picture.   The growing pressure of population upon land resources will force some reconsideration of the nature of these soils.
Thus, though the best soils in currently populated regions may be
clearly better than any in the Ceja de la Montana, the low Selva, or
the llanos, there are soil resources in this region which are likely
to be equal to, or better than, those available for cultivation to the
people who will form the bulk of the colonists.

In a larger context, the essential requirement for rapid development of tropical agriculture is the finding of commercial export
crops. That is the lesson of the tropical coast of Ecuador, which
was part of the tropical agriculture frontier a generation ago.
About this area, experts had doubts. Reports written as late as
the middle 1940's spoke of the deterrent effects of the heavy rainfall, the rapid overgrowth of underbrush, the lack of labor, the
unlikelihood that Sierra Indians would move into such regions,
the difficulty of building roads on infirm soils, and especially
the need for a crop which could overcome the hazards of cultivation. That crop--bananas--had been found by the 1950's and the
rest is history. It is useful, therefore, to keep in mind that future changes in techniques, in demand, and in supply may make
for changes in evaluation of possible benefits.

One additional feature of the Ecuador coast experience needs
stressing. It is that though even now the land available for banana culture in Ecuador is not equal in quality or in location to
the best on the Mosquito Coast in Central America, changes a-
long the Caribbean due to weather, the using up of the best lands,
political conditions, and the like, brought Ecuador's lands within
the production horizon. Thus, it was not so much that conditions
had changed in Ecuador but that growing demands elsewhere for
tropical lands led to a search for new supplies. Beyond national
boundaries can arise market factors which may give an entirely
different turn to events in this region. In the largest possible
context, the demand for, and the supply of, tropical lands for
agriculture will be affected by the worldwide pressure for increasing the ability of the land to produce foods, fiber, and fuel
for human consumption.

GROWTH PATTERN OF THE ANDEAN NATIONS

The Andean nations have grown in recent years by expanding their
export sectors. This has meant that economic development has
been concentrated largely in particular areas where resources
could support expanding export production (Table V). In the case
of Colombia, this involved the expansion of areas and crops long
of importance. Coffee production, for example, provided the
sharp increase in foreign-exchange earnings which have financed
in large measure the development experienced since World War II.
In Ecuador, new crops and new areas figured importantly in the
economic development process. In most cases, infrastructure

TABLE V

Comparison of Growth Rates, Major Indicators

	Colombia	Ecuador	Peru	Bolivia
Income per capita, 1961	$373	$223	$269	$122
Growth rates, GNP	4.9	6.0	4.2	0.8
Growth rate, population	2.8	2.3	2.0	2.2
Growth rate, exports	2.1	9.0	8.0	0.7
Exports as per cent of GNP	13.5	22.1	19.1	23.4
Major Export	Coffee	Bananas	Cotton	Tin
Relative importance (per cent)	75.0	42.0	20.0	71.0
Areas affected by exports	Pacific Valleys	Coast	Coast	Altiplano
Differentials: developed vs. underdeveloped regions	5-1	4-1	12-1	-

investments have been concentrated in the growth areas to bring about an increase in productivity of the export activity and, therefore, an increase in the inflow of development funds.

An examination of the changing economic position of each Andean nation during the past war will reveal the effects of such a development policy. Bolivia, which has seen the least growth in gross domestic product, has nonetheless continued to emphasize export activities. It was the weakness in both the demand for its principal exports and their prices which prevented the export sector from providing the growth anticipated. Yet whatever growth that did occur may be traced to exports. Ecuador, which might have found itself in the same position as Bolivia because of the weakness of the market for cacao and rice, was able to avoid a slowdown by a shift to bananas and the exploitation of new soil resources. Ecuador has been able, therefore, to post relatively rapid domestic product gains consistently, but the gains have been largely in the provinces of the coast.

Peru's situation has grown increasingly favorable since the 1950's as her exports, the range of exports, and the growth rate of domestic products increased. But almost all of this growth, like that of Ecuador, has been limited to the coast. Only in Colombia, where many economic regions centered about aggressive cities that have for some time been following independent growth paths, was there any lessening in concentration of economic activity in particular regions. Even so, the development in the postwar period did not see new areas or major new export crops developed.

In all of these cases, the degree of export concentration and the dependence on export earnings point up the dependence of economic development on a relatively narrow basis. Experience has demonstrated in Latin America the essential weakness for the longer pull of such development policies, a weakness that is only temporarily obviated by resort to new crops to replace the old as principal dollar-earners. Moreover, concentration has meant that the differentials in per capita incomes among regions within each country have been widened, creating a politically dangerous situation.

GROWTH STRATEGIES

In each country, development planners have to decide between a
course which has meant more intensive use of existing cultivable
and settled areas or the extension of the economic resource horizon. In the absence of an interconnecting Carretera Marginal de
la Selva, which will bring some 7,400,000 hectares into effective
economic utilization, the decisions tended to favor coastal regions,
especially in Ecuador and Peru, and the already settled areas of
Colombia. Only in Bolivia has it become apparent that the Oriente
must play a major role if over-all standards of living are to be
raised.

The highway then broadens the planning context. For Ecuador,
where rapid tropical agricultural growth has forced the bringing
into cultivation of from 150,000 to 400,000 new hectares since
1954, and where at that rate most developable land on the coast
will be under cultivation by 1975, the highway will make possible
the use of an area as large as the entire coast and thus permit
economic growth to continue at somewhat near the present favorable rate.

For Peru, where incorporation of more coastal land means heavy
investments in irrigation and where already there is a general
shift from crops and other land uses with lower yields to much
higher yields in export commodities, the highway will make possible the satisfaction of growing national demand for food, fiber,
and forest products without using up limited foreign exchange. For
meat and lumber, for building and furniture, the situation is already crucial. In an Oriente supplied with adequate low-cost transport, Peru can find the elements making for advantageous internal
development.

The case of Colombia, although complicated by a number of growth
points--Cali, Medellin, Bogota, Bucaramanga, and Baranquilla,
for example--reveals the essential choice between doing better,
and therefore more intensively, what is being done and extending
the production frontier. The location of the llanos relatively close
to settled areas and the violencia of recent years have made for
rather more development in the Oriente than might otherwise have
been expected.

IMPROVED NATIONAL TRANSPORT NETWORKS

The Carretera Marginal de la Selva will bring substantial indirect benefits through improving the interconnectivity of the transport system, making possible a more balanced economic growth process and, equally important, political integration. In the international context, the Carretera lays the basis for a more effective common market.

The Pacific Coast and Andean countries of Latin America are still largely economic beachheads. Few areas have been settled and these have had special advantages in climate or transport for many centuries. The main transport link remains the ocean and thus the most traveled routes for trade lead outward to North America and Europe. From the ports at Lima, Guayaquil, Buenaventura, and Matarani, for example, penetration routes reach in to tap specific regions which either serve as production areas for export commodities or provide a supply hinterland for the port itself. Here and there in the Andes are communities which have grown self-sufficiently while others have broken through the geographic barriers which had limited them to an autarkic existence to become important in regional, national, and even international trade.

The existing system of transport, then, is a series of grids based on major ports of entry or valley production centers. Lima and the Peruvian network serve to illustrate one type of Andean transport system, while that based on Cali, Medellin, and Bogota points up the qualities of the other type of system.

While it is true that geography dictates the nature of the Peruvian network, the exact location of the heart of the system was a choice made by the Spanish. In so doing, they replaced the Cuzco-oriented Inca road network, which was inward-looking and designed to link distant valley provinces to the imperial capital, with a network looking outward, designed to provide for the flow of trade to Spain and to give political control from the port. Though the rule of Spain has long since ended, little has been added to this system, either in routes or in concept.

Given this network, it is not surprising that Lima remains, and grows even more, as the center of all economic activity. But continued centralization means that the gap between the level of development in Lima and that in its various hinterlands will widen.

By contrast, because the coasts of Colombia are tropical, the Spanish chose the temperate-zone Andean valleys for their capital and subsidiary cities. Transport's first task was to link these cities to the nearest port on the Atlantic or Pacific. Its second was to link each city with the exploitable hinterland in the valleys and adjacent areas. Because some of these valleys, the Gran Sabana of Bogota, for example, were large and potentially rich, transport linkage advanced but little beyond this stage until the development of export crops, mainly coffee. In addition to making necessary substantial improvements in the city-to-port systems, the need arose also from 1940 on for a linkage system between the main cities, especially those in the Central Triangle. The Colombian system involving heavy use of air cargo and transport facilities, as well as riverways, roads, and railways, is more "advanced" than that of Peru because of emergence of many nodes.

Ecuador, with its Guayaquil-Quito axis and local grids based on it, and Bolivia, with its linkage system for La Paz and the main Altiplano towns and a spinal connection to the Pacific Coast, are variations of the Peruvian and Colombian systems. But as each system stands, only the basic linkage needs have been met. The Carretera Marginal de la Selva breaks with the penetration linkage system and provides interconnection alternatives to both oceans and reaches and ties into the region, nation, and, indeed, continental economic systems areas which until now have been effectively barred from full participation in economic development.

Economic growth, in order to spread more evenly from the centers of concentration, requires a transport linkage system with the costs of moving freight and passengers brought low enough to remove the advantages of concentration. Regions with lower land and labor costs can begin to compete effectively. What the Carretera Marginal does, by completing the networks and orienting them away from serving merely as penetration grids, is to make possible a spillover of rapid growth activity to other areas. The successive effects of this spillover process serve to bring all regions into a national growth process which brings about balanced development.

The role of the Carretera Marginal de la Selva is both permissive, in that it makes possible the elimination of regional differentials, and compulsive, in that it forces a realignment of the use of resources, bringing into play new regions, resources, and economic relationships.

INTERNAL POLITICAL INTEGRATION

No nation can long permit large areas within its borders to remain beyond effective control, if for no other reason than that these distant regions represent a drain upon the national treasury as well as a constant threat of passing out of national control. The history of each of the Andean countries has shown clearly the essential truth of this possibility. Thus, whether the cost is great or small, nations must undertake expenditures which have as their purpose the integration of the national territories. The Carretera Marginal de la Selva in this light is an instrument for political integration and is the more effective because it will be accompanied by economic development.

The fact that this is not a highway which reaches out from an established base to unoccupied territory, but one which parallels existing networks and ties an entire region together, providing it with access to all sections of the national territory, gives the Carretera Marginal substantial utility as a means for political control. Far larger reaches of the Oriente can be brought under political control from many points in the developed regions of the Andes than from the centers of the penetration road system.

Political integration, too, is more effective when the new regions are able in large measure to support their own growth. Brought to the level of effective political and economic development by the Carretera Marginal de la Selva, the different provinces and departments in the Oriente will become in reality integral parts of Colombia, Ecuador, Peru, and Bolivia.

There is an additional advantage in this political integration which is sure to come from the highway. To the extent that nations no longer feel themselves threatened at weak points along their borders, a basis can be laid for peaceful relations among them. Conscious that every region is embarked upon the kind of development that will leave no point exposed to possible adverse

action by foreign powers, continental or extracontinental, governments can enter more fully into programs for common markets
or other forms of international economic integration.

LATIN AMERICAN COMMON MARKET

The decision of Latin American nations to form a common market to increase the pace and the scale of economic development
has important implications for the projection of transport requirements on the South American continent. Though there has been a
steady increase in intracontinental trade, still less than 11% of
all foreign commerce is accounted for by such movements. In the
decade from 1950 to 1960 Latin American export trade to the
rest of the world increased 17%. [3] By regions, the increase was
as follows:

	%
United States	8
Latin America	10
Western Europe	25

The percentage participation by region in the growth of Latin
American exports from 1950 to 1960 was:

United States	22
Latin America	10
Western Europe	42

And trade between countries remains difficult. Yet the success
of economic development for Bolivia, Colombia, Ecuador, and
Peru, as well as for other Latin American nations, lies in the possibility of opening markets larger than those available domestically.

The actions taken thus far to implement the Treaty of Montevideo
have been largely limited to tariff reduction and other similar pro-
cedural matters. But the Carretera Marginal de la Selva represents the largest single common market transport project and will
provide, when completed, a land route with relatively low operating
costs which will be a major link between participating nations. This
project is an example of the regional approach to transport planning
necessary to broaden the development horizon of Latin American
nations.

Strictly speaking, the trade flow between nations in the common market and along the Carretera Marginal de la Selva, will be determined by the relative advantages each nation has in trade. But it must be added that such advantages are not simply comparisons among nations but among regions, some of which extend beyond national borders. Table VI, comparing the expected annual rate of growth for some crops which can be and are being grown in the region with the rate of income growth, indicates that in almost all cases by 1975 the area under cultivation will have to have increased faster than per capita income and purchasing power. Such growth necessarily means a resort to new production areas. The growth rates refer only to domestic consumption and do not include exports, which would push the rates up further.

TABLE VI
Expected Annual Growth in Latin American Consumption

Crop	Growth per cent
Rice	1. 88
Cacao	2. 32
Cotton	2. 82
Beef	2. 04
Bananas	1. 76
Coffee	2. 11
Income, per capita(1945-1961)	1. 9

Source: The Latin American Common Market, United Nations, 1959, pp. 78-83.

This new highway will be opening up for development an area the true potential of which can only be guessed at. But since each of the three main geographical provinces through which it passes-- the llanos (sabanas lands), the Ceja de la Montana (semitropical piedmont ranging from wet to arid), and the selva (wet jungle river basin land)--is in some sense quite different from areas now in agricultural production in Latin America, it is reasonable to expect important elements of comparative advantage to be present.

Already portions of this area which have been opened by highway investments have brought about shifts in production from former areas. Sugar in Santa Cruz (Bolivia) has reduced that nation's

dependence on imports.   Cattle in the Colombian llanos, coffee
in Peruvian montana, tea in the Ecuadorian Oriente--each represents the emerging advantage of the region.

Substantial, though unmeasured, amounts of contraband move
across the borders of Colombia (into and from Venezuela and
Ecuador), [4] Ecuador (into and from Colombia and Peru), Peru
(into and from Ecuador, Bolivia, Brazil, and Colombia), and
Bolivia (into and from Peru, Brazil, and Argentina) in the general region served by the highway.   Since the contraband now being transported does not in fact move great distances, representing
largely the normal interchange of goods between adjacent regions
differing both in natural endowment and in income and rates of exchange, its existence is a measure of the likely impact of the highway.   Put another way, the highway may have little immediate
effect on the trade from Lima to Bogota, but substantial effect
on the movement from the Colombian llanos to the Ecuadorian
sierra, or from the Peruvian department of Madre de Dios to La
Paz, Bolivia.   Thus, even though from a national viewpoint trade
did not increase a good deal, for the regions affected the movement would be relatively large and of significance for the development of the total area through which the Carretera Marginal de la
Selva passes.

Special provisions have been made in the Treaty of Montevideo
for the position of the "less-developed nations" in Latin America,
such as Bolivia and Ecuador.   It is precisely these nations which
must continue to expand their exports of basic commodities and to
widen the range of their production in order to be able to partici-
pate effectively in the common market.   The system of preferences
for the small nations was designed to create conditions which would
attract capital for the development of their domestic investment,
including the Carretera Marginal de la Selva, which leads to providing new areas for production as well as new export and domestic consumption commodities, and to enhance these preferences.

But no one nation is in fact a single region with a single rate of
growth.   In the case of Bolivia, Colombia, Ecuador, and Peru,
there are those areas which are in some sense "central" and those
which are in the periphery.   By increasing the effect of the growth
impulse from the center, the Carretera Marginal will permit the
spilling over of growth from the center.   The experience of Venezuela, where vast highway investments have been permitting the

opening up of large, previously distant regions, indicates that
the spillover process is speeded up rapidly by highway investment and leads to a significant reduction in regional income and
development differentials. It is also true that the whole common
market has its centers and its peripheries so that for all the nations the role of the Carretera Marginal de la Selva will be to
encourage spillover and the reduction of differentials in rates of
development.

The Carretera Marginal de la Selva and its expected impact
upon the emerging Latin American Common Market can be judged
not only in terms of the transport requirements for development,
but also in terms of the expected changes in the consumption of
foods, fibers, and fuel in the member nations in the years ahead.
The highway will enable nations to meet expected demands and at
the same time will serve to bring about more balanced development of all the common market member nations and of regions
within each nation.

DIRECT COSTS

Colombia

The direct cost of the highway is twofold. First, there are the
construction costs of the right-of-way and structures, mainly
bridges (Table VII). In addition, there are development costs,
including feeder roads, extension services, land surveys, colonization aids, and the like. It was not possible to forecast these
costs as effectively as construction costs. Where possible, as
in the case of Colombia, these estimated development costs are
based upon extrapolations of Ministry of Agriculture data, a
standard cost per farm family was applied. However calculated,
the development costs (even if not borne directly by the highway
construction agency--normally the government) are to be sub-
tracted from gross benefits to obtain net benefits and represent
the costs in the highway necessary to bring agricultural production up to predicted levels.

A major indirect cost of the Carretera Marginal de la Selva for
Colombia, Ecuador, Peru, and Bolivia is the cost of the alternative highway investments possible. While it is not possible to
know this alternative cost in detail, it is possible to determine--

TABLE VII

Summary of Costs of Carretera Marginal de la Selva (U.S. Dollars)

	Colombia	Ecuador	Peru	Bolivia
Construction	74,300,000	53,500,000	174,700,000	50,800,000
Development Costs	38,800,000	27,800,000	53,100,000	21,000,000

by extrapolation of past experience, by examination of country plans, or by some combination of these--what funds will be available, what has in some general or specific way been committed to new construction in the years ahead, and what relation the proposed expenditure on the Carretera Marginal de la Selva has to these sums. This permits a general statement as to whether the new highway can in fact be built with or without recourse to large new sources of funds. For each nation, therefore, we provide an analysis of budgets and plans against the background of which we present the new highway.

Colombia will have available from internal and international sources some $3.2 billion for public investment purposes in the period 1965-74. This estimate, as shown in Table VIII, is based upon an extrapolation of current income and expenditure trends as well as upon the Plan Cuatrienal de Inversiones Publicas Nacionales. Using the same basis, it is estimated that Colombia will spend $673 million for highway construction in that same period. At least $173 million of this has been recommended for high priority projects through 1971,[5] and additional unknown amounts are currently being committed. The highway costs of the Colombia portion of the Carretera Marginal, or $74.3 million, represent about 11% of the expected ten-year highway budget. This suggests that the alternative, or indirect, cost of the proposed highway will be relatively low. The fact that the Plan for Improvements in National Transportation includes projects in the settled heart of the country only, all of which have been assigned high priority, emphasizes this relationship.

Ecuador

Ecuador's planning authorities have set aside $342 million in the next ten years for highway expenditures. Of this amount, a recent transport survey team[6] recommended that $93 million be spent on high priority projects, largely on the coast. More than $47 million has already been financed. The Carretera Marginal represents 15.6% of funds available for highway construction between 1964 and 1973 (Table IX). A decision to build the Carretera Marginal need not mean a postponing of essential highway construction in key export production areas. It is, however, useful to note the high dependence in the ten-year capital budget upon available international sources of funds.

TABLE VIII

Projection of Availability of Funds for Colombian Highway Construction, 1961-74 (1960 U.S. Dollars in Millions)

	1961	1962	1963	1964	1965-69	1970-74
Gross government current income	243.3	266.1	284.8	304.7	1,875.3	2,627.8
Gross government administrative expenditures	169.6	175.6	181.6	188.0	1,043.4	1,239.2
Government administrative surplus	73.7	90.5	103.2	116.7	831.9	1,388.6
Other internal sources	42.6	25.3	19.7	19.9	141.4	236.1
Total internal sources	116.3	115.8	122.9	136.6	972.3	1,624.7
External sources	52.6	55.1	57.6	60.1	300.6	350.7
Total Available	168.9	170.9	180.5	196.7	1,272.9	1,975.4
Highway investment	42.0	42.0	42.4	44.3	263.9	409.3
Total Cost of Carretera Marginal de la Selva				74.3		
Carretera Marginal de la Selva as per cent of Highway Funds, 1965-74				11.0		

Sources: Plan Cuatrenial de Inversiones Publicas Nacionales, 1961-74; Plan for Improvements in National Transportation; Plan General de Desarrollo Economico y Social.

TABLE IX
Projection of Availability of Funds for Ecuadorian Highway Construction
(1960 U.S. Dollars in Millions)

	1957-62 Actual	1964-68 Projected*	1969-73 Projected*
Public investment funds available	252.8	383.8	590.5
International funds available		273.8+	332.8+
Highway expenditures	73.8	129.0	212.9
New Highway construction (assumed to be 67% of highway expenditure)		86.4	142.6
Cost in Ecuador of Carretera Marginal de la Selva		53.5	
Cost of Carretera Marginal as per cent of highway funds available, 1964-73		15.6	

*Based upon plan requirements

+Estimates by JNP

Sources: Plan General de Desarrollo Economico y Social, Libros 1 y 2 (Quito: Junta Nacional de Planificacion y Coordinacion Economica, 1963); Memoria, Banco Central del Ecuador, 1962, 1963; National Transportation Study--Ecuador, (Quito: Parsons, Brinckerhoff, Quade, and Douglas, 1964).

135

Peru

For Peru (where as currently planned, some $2.7 billion will be
available for public investment projects in the period 1964-76)
apart from the assigning of priorities no serious problems in
financing and constructing the Carretera Marginal de la Selva
are foreseen.   The proposed highway represents 6.4% of the
public investment budget.   Some 83% of the planned financing
is internal, continuing a trend characteristic of postwar
Peru.

Of the public investment budget, a relatively modest 13%--
about $200 million--has been set aside for the Plan Vial, 1964-
1971.

A similar allocation of funds would make almost as much available between 1972 and 1976.   Of the total now planned for highway construction through 1976, the cost of the Carretera Marginal is some 44% of available funds (Table X).

A continuation of the current financing procedures implies a need
for about $118 million from international sources from 1964 to
1976, half of which could be used to begin construction of the
Carretera Marginal de la Selva.   In any case, the Plan Vial is
being restudied, as is the whole public investment budget, on
the basis of new priorities which will assign the Carretera Marginal a more significant role in Peruvian transport planning.

Bolivia

The indirect cost of the highway in Bolivia is high.   In view of
current resources and projected availability of external financing, it is evident that a decision to build all the Carretera Marginal sections within the next 15 years would require a rather
complete reassessment of priorities.   Some $105.7 million are
now planned for construction and improvement of highways.   Of
this amount, assuming continuation of the recent practice of
financing 10% of such outlays from internal sources, about $11
million will be provided from limited capital funds.   The remainder
is expected to be drawn from grants and loans (Table XI).   It is
probable, therefore, that a beginning on the Carretera Marginal
de la Selva in Bolivia cannot be made until the middle 1970's
in the absence of substantial changes in national highway planning
and availability of sources.

TABLE X

Projection of Availability of Funds for Peruvian Highway Construction
(1960 U.S. Dollars in Millions)

	1962-63 Actual	1964-67 Projected	1968-71 Projected	1972-76 Projected
Public Investment	247.8	600.1	784.8	1,332.4
Internal public investment funds available	205.7	498.1	631.4	1,106.0
Highway construction	35.2	107.6*	91.9*	197.2+
Internal financing of highway construction	5.6	50.4*	84.7*	143.8+
Anticipated cost of Carretera Marginal de la Selva		174.7		
Carretera Marginal as per cent of highway funds, 1964-76		44.0		

*Based on Plan Vial
+Extrapolation based on 1962-71 average relationships

Sources: Plan Vial, 1962-1971; Programa de Inversiones Publicas, 1964-65; Analisis de la realidad Socio-Economica del Peru, Problemas Financieras.

137

TABLE XI

Availability of Funds for Bolivian Highway Construction, 1965-79
(1960 U.S. Dollars in Millions)

	1965-70	1971-74	1975-79
Government income*	220.2	307.8	354.7
Available for capital expenditures+	11.1	15.5	17.8
Proposed Highway construction expenditures++	46.6	37.8	21.3
External loans and grants+++	41.9	34.0	19.1

Cost of Carretera Marginal de la Selva   50.0

*Based on extrapolation of Plan Bienal, 1963-64, assumed 9.5% of gross domestic
   product.
+Assumed 5.2% of government expenditures.
++Based on cost estimates and priorities in Plan General de Desarrollo, 1961.
+++Assumes Bienal Plan practice of providing internal finance for 10% of highway
   cost is continued.

Table XII presents a summary of the benefits anticipated from the construction of the Carretera Marginal de la Selva. It also ranks these benefits in order of importance from the point of view of economic development planning for each nation through which the highway passes. An A means that the benefit listed is of primary importance in achieving economic growth in the nation as well as in the zone of influence. That is, the highway will have a direct and significant impact upon national growth rates of and by itself.

A B indicates that the Carretera Marginal is but one of several elements needed to obtain significant changes in the extrapolated growth path. This growth path is, in turn, a reflection of what will happen in the absence of major structural changes in the national economy.

Finally, a C suggests that the highway will not, of itself or even in conjunction with other major projects, push the economy from the extrapolated growth represented by the benefit indicator.

Necessarily, such rankings are in part intuitive though they are based upon, and are in fact, a summary of our evaluation procedures. They indicate that for each country--Colombia, Ecuador, Peru, and Bolivia--the over-all benefits are such as to bring about a significant improvement in the growth potential and, therefore, the economic development processes.

The burden and cost of the proposed highway varies according to the availability of both internal and external financing, planning objectives, and priority rankings of each nation as well as to the relation of total cost of the highway to the increase in Gross National Product expected from its construction. In Table XIII cost burdens are summarized for Colombia, Ecuador, Peru, and Bolivia. Only in the case of Bolivia is there any substantial change in construction planning, obtaining of financing, and indeed in the working out of investment priorities presented. For the other nations, the highway is a feasible objective requiring minor changes in planning and financing. When these costs are compared with expected benefits, it may be concluded that the highway will yield over-all benefits in a development planning context well in excess of costs.

TABLE XII

Summary of Benefits from Carretera Marginal de la Selva

	Colombia	Ecuador	Peru	Bolivia
DIRECT BENEFITS				
Increase in gross agricultural production	B	C	A	A
Increase in per capita farm income, region, and nation	C	C	B	A
Increase in population absorption capacity	B	B	A	A
Increase in cultivable area	B	A	A	A
Increase in range of agricultural production	C	B	A	A
INDIRECT BENEFITS				
Improves political integration	B	A	A	A
Improves interconnectivity of transport system	B	B	A	A
Aids balanced growth	A	B	A	A
Widens inter-Latin American markets bringing benefits from common market	A	A	A	A
Reduces international tensions	B	A	A	B
SUMMARY EVALUATION	B	B	A	A

A = CMS an essential element in improving economic growth.

B = CMS with other elements will improve economic growth.

C = Represents no significant change from plan extrapolations in absence of highway.

140

TABLE XIII

Measuring the Burden of the Cost of Constructing the Carretera Marginal de la Selva

	Colombia	Ecuador	Peru	Bolivia
DIRECT COSTS				
Construction	B	A	B	C
Development	A	B	A	A
INDIRECT COSTS				
Internal financing	A	B	A	C
External financing	B	B	B	C
SUMMARY EVALUATION	A-B	B	A-B	C

A = No significant burden or basic change in over-all priorities.
B = Minor changes in general public investment and highway priorities.
C = Substantial changes in investment priorities.

141

APPENDIX

In the text of this chapter, we have outlined in broad and general
terms the benefits and costs of the Carretera Marginal de la
Selva, attempting in summary an evaluation of the impact of the
highway upon each of the nations through which it will pass--
Colombia, Ecuador, Peru, and Bolivia. However, back of this
general evaluation was a much more specific evaluation, section by section, of the highway. This was done by the engineers
and economists associated with the project in order to provide a
basis for determining for each nation the order of priority of
each possible section.

Though Peru, for example, has decided that the construction of
the highway is in the national interest after having considered
the gross benefits as compared with the gross costs, there still
remains the problem of how and where to begin the construction,
apart from the naïve conclusion "at the beginning." What was
worked out then was an evaluation index, which we chose to call
a "priority index." Essentially, it can be defined as the average
annual net income to be received from economic activities developed along the particular highway section as a percentage of
the total cost including highway construction and development.

Obviously, the average annual net increase in income will be a
part of the Gross Domestic Product at the time it is recorded.
We are concerned with the increase over any income now being
generated along the highway section under study because we want
to measure what the highway can be expected to do that could not
be done in some other way without the highway. Moreover, because the majority of the areas through which the highway passes
now has little or no development and because for Peru and the
other nations along the highway there is underemployment of
many resources, gross and net additions to domestic product will
be approximately equal. Add to this the fact that agricultural production, once begun, will likely mean little import or diversion of
resources from other parts of the nation.

The only major subtraction that needs to be made from the additions to income or product is that arising from the cost of maintenance of the highway and ancillary facilities.

The priority index is thus a rate of return on the investment in the
Carretera Marginal de la Selva for each section. But it has a

further interesting characteristic. Time is not taken explicitly
into consideration. Instead, production estimates are worked
out for the area under study for that period when the highway is
in full use. This permits us to compare sections which will be
completed at various stages in the future without having to take
into account a discount rate implied by the passage of time. With
the priority index, the ultimate yields of all the sections planned
can be put beside each other to determine the order of construction which is preferable without consideration of the varied time
horizons which distort such a comparison in favor of the sections
with the shortest likely time horizon.

We can, of course, move from the priority index to an actual
net yield on investment by the application of the appropriate interest rate, life, and residual value of the facility. However,
the index cannot be used to compare sections in Peru with those
in Ecuador or Bolivia, for example, since there is an implicit
reckoning of the individual nation's domestic product in the priority index. Moreover, there is an implicit reckoning of the
changes in population and other market conditions within the national frontiers.

Note that this priority index does not take road-user benefits
directly into account, so it tends to underestimate the long-range
benefits to accrue from the Carretera Marginal de la Selva. Not
much attention is paid to the possibility of industrial development
along the highway, attention being paid specifically to agriculture.
Nor is any attempt made to take into account the possible and even
probable changes in agricultural productivity. Rather, current
farm sizes, practices, and labor utilization ratios have been used.
Lastly, but by no means of less importance, is the fact that the
benefits apply to a predetermined zone of probable influence which
may well be conservative.

All of this means that priority indexes can be and have been worked
out using existing information, scarce as it is, which will nonetheless permit a distinction without respect to the order of development of regions within a nation. To be sure, these indexes need
review constantly, as development proceeds, to assure that no new
information becoming available later is ignored in the continuing
determination of priorities.

In short, what such an evaluation index does is to permit the national planner to make rational choices in terms of current horizons

among the various sections of the highway.   Yet to be worked out is a priority index which permits national planners to put all their possible projects into some context of comparability so that an efficient use can be made of the scarce material resources of developing nations.   But along this line progress can be made.

Notes to Chapter 4

[1] This chapter appeared as an article in the Traffic Quarterly, April, 1966. Permission to use material in this book has been graciously granted.

[2] Helpful comments by Eric Dodge and Lorand Dabasi-Schweng are gratefully acknowledged. The figures for which no sources are cited are estimates prepared by the author or are those of Eric Dodge, Lorand Dabasi-Schweng, or Hans Platenius. They represent what we consider to be the best approximations in view of very limited data. At the very least, they do suggest correct comparable magnitudes.

[3] El Desarrollo Economico de America Latina en la Postguerra (Mexico City: Economic Commission for Latin America, 1963).

[4] For an analysis of contraband problems in the frontier zone between Venezuela and Colombia, see "Posibilidades de Integracion de las Zonas Fronterizas Colombia-Venezuela, " Bank for International Development, April, 1964.

[5] See Ministry of Public Works, Plan for Improvements in National Transportation (Bogota: Parsons, Brinckerhoff, Quade, and Douglas, 1961), p. 1178.

[6] National Transportation Study--Ecuador (Quito: Parsons, Brinckerhoff, Quade, and Douglas, 1964).

CHAPTER **5** TRANSPORT
INVESTMENT
STRATEGY IN
LATIN AMERICA

TRANSPORT INVESTMENT
STRATEGY IN LATIN AMERICA

Transport investments typically are very large ones. The opportunity for serious mistakes is great indeed. More important, the cost to the nation of a wasteful transport investment is not simply the failure of the new highway, harbor improvement, railway or air facility to yield the expected returns, whether in direct or indirect benefits. It is the loss of an opportunity to have used the expended funds in far better ways, to much more fruitful effect, in some other investment whether in the transport field or not.

THE NATURE OF TRANSPORT STRATEGIES

The essence of an effective transport investment strategy[1] for a developing nation is that the specific project must have a measurable impact upon the pace of economic development in that nation. One may speak of a demand strategy or a supply strategy. In the Venezuelan Tejerias-Valencia autopista case, we have a good example of a demand strategy. There, every demand indicator--traffic counts, maintenance costs, and the like--pointed up the need for more capacity in transport facilities between the Caracas area and the Aragua valley. The problem was to select that potential transport project from among the several available which would meet that demand and meet it in such a way as to lower transport costs and/or increase the general productivity of the region served. A demand strategy is an effective response to an established transport need.

However, demand strategies are likely to be rare in developing nations. Seldom does the pressure build up so greatly that it becomes apparent to almost all observers in and out of government that something must be done. Obviously, the task of determining how to evaluate the results of a demand strategy is not an extremely difficult one.

By contrast, a supply strategy is rather more tentative and difficult. The decision to build the Atlantic Railway in Colombia may be taken as an example of a supply strategy. We call it supply strategy because the purpose is to provide a mode of transport which will either lead to the creation of a traffic flow not previously existent in the region to be served or which will shift a pre-existing traffic flow from some other route or mode thought to be less advantageous. Thus a transport facility is provided in

149

advance of firm evidence of demand with the intention that it
will lead to the creation of the demand.

Needless to say, such strategies are much more risky, though
far more common in Latin America and elsewhere in the developing[2] world.   The essence of a good supply strategy is the choice
of the correct transport or other investment project.   Correctness
is to be measured in the terms of the net gain in measurable aggregate demand over aggregate cost.   But there is more to this
choice than that.   Whereas most demand strategies will involve
relatively simple alternatives and less complex patterns of inter-
dependence--at least at the time of the choice--supply strategies
frequently require careful study of possible interdependence.

The Atlantic Railway in Colombia runs from Puerto Berrio, where
it makes a connection[3] with the Pacific Railway via Medellin and
with the Gran Sabana network via La Dorada to Bogota, to Santa
Marta on the Caribbean coast.   It parallels the Magdalena River
which has served for many generations as the principal transport
route north from Central Colombia.   But unlike the river, the
railway does not lead to either of the traditional Caribbean ports,
Barranquilla, or Cartagena.   In addition to providing through
transit for goods moving to and from the coast, it was intended
that the railway play some role in generating land settlement and
agricultural use in the vast Magdalena valley through which it
passes.   Thus the test of this supply strategy was to be not simply
any saving of time or cost over the existing Magdalena riverway--
because of reduction in transfer of goods from one mode to another or because of removal of the factor of seasonality because
of changing water levels in the river-- but even more the resultant growth in the aggregate demand of the nation as hitherto
unused or underused resources came into play.   To be sure, it
was also to be the link that created out of a number of "pieces"
a national railway system for whatever advantages the existence
of such a system might provide.   Thus far into the 1960's it has
not been established that the Atlantic Railway has played enough
of a role in increasing aggregate demand to a sufficient level to
permit the recovery of its cost.   While it may be too early to
judge the effectiveness of this strategy, there is a reasonable
doubt that it was the correct one in view of the circumstances.

Ecuador's transport planning will give a better example of a
series of supply strategies in action.   The Ten Year Plan 1964-73

envisages a major emphasis on improving agricultural output
and thus export. The purpose of the plan was to spell out and
provide answers for all those problems which might deter the
needed increase in agricultural productivity. The plan proposed the projects thought necessary to permit a rapid increase
in exportable crops. Ecuador planners assumed that exports
would increase the aggregate demand of the nation, pushing up
the level of national income and of per capita income. Every
project, then, was to be judged by its contribution to this objective. The extent to which each project made possible the early
recovery of its cost was to be a key factor in determining its
priority. During the first five years, then, most highway projects were to be undertaken in the Guayas River valley and the
coastal region in general. In the later period, efforts were to
be taken to spread the benefits of the economic growth, to remove bottlenecks as they appeared and to relieve population
pressures, especially in the Sierra of the Andes. Among other
things, this would involve colonization of areas to be opened by
highway projects.

The highway projects came first, not because they are easy to
build, or because international financing was readily available,
but because they were considered essential in the achievement
of all other aspects of the plan. They "supplied" the transport
capacity foreseen as necessary for the planned increase in agricultural production. They were not, however, the only elements
in this over-all development strategy because along with highways
went agricultural extension, research, improvements in marketing structure, education, docking facilities in Guayaquil, and
the vehicle fleet.

In contrast with the Colombian transport planning where at least
some of the reasoning which led to the construction of the Atlantic
Railway assumed[4] that, per se, a complete railway network was
better than improving intermodal connections; and where little
went into the provision of the elements for the development of
the Magdalena Valley, the Ecuador plan considered transport as
key supply elements in an interdependent relationship leading to
an over-all improvement in national income and in its distribution.

PROBLEMS IN THE SELECTION OF TRANS-
PORT STRATEGIES AND INVESTMENT PLANNING

The distinction between a demand and a supply strategy points
up the need for an understanding both of the role to be played by
each transport investment in the over-all economic development
of a nation and of the need for careful measurement of the expected results of the transport strategy. Transport investment
planning has as its purpose the efficient allocation of the community's resources with a view to maximizing the return on
these resources in the light of the announced economic and political objectives. First come the objectives, to be determined by
the people themselves. Then comes the allocation of the resources
but within the context of a plan which sets forth a means of measuring the various possible outcomes in terms of the plan itself.
The plan, too, indicates which projects best accomplish the
national objectives.

Harral[5] has noted that there are at least six problems in transport investment planning which merit consideration. First,
there is a significant difference between the cost of the resources
to the transport agency and the opportunity costs of those same resources to the nation. The resources to be used, of course, are
the labor, the land, and the finance. All of these, in developing
nations, are very likely to be selling in the market at prices below what they could earn in their best use. The possible excep-
tion is the level of wages of unskilled labor which is often higher
than would be obtained in a perfect market. The consequence is
that it may appear to be cheaper to build a highway, a railway, a
harbor improvement, or develop an air transport service than
in fact it is. The discrepancies will begin to show up as the pace
of development increases when it will become increasingly
apparent that there are bottlenecks and misallocations. Moreover, these will indicate that a different order of priorities
would have been established had the opportunity costs of the resources been taken into account. On the other hand, the concept
of opportunity costs requires that there be some alternative use
now or in the future of the available resources. Because it will
not always be apparent that such uses exist or that if they exist
they can be taken into consideration in the urgency of the moment,
great care must be taken to insure an objective study of opportunity costs, usually not by the transport planning office itself.

The second problem is that of the sunk costs of pre-existing investments. The fact that a railway right-of-way is currently in existence so that for low additional expenditures it can be expanded or converted may be irrelevant for the transport decision to be faced. In Argentina, where substantial investment in a massive network of railways exists, perhaps too much attention has been given to this network to the exclusion of alternatives. One study of the Argentine transport situation, for example, has concluded that it would be more economical to abandon the railway, regardless of the investment involved and to build parallel highways, rather than rehabilitate and operate the rail system. The point is that sunk investments have no or very little opportunity cost. They must either be employed in their current or slightly modified form or be abandoned. They are therefore irrelevant to the current investment decision. Obviously, though, when a rail system exists, there also exist organized firms with management, laborers, their know-how, their interrelated marketing structures, and their available political pressure to protect their survival.

In the third place, often not enough attention is paid to the totality of investments necessary to make a particular transport strategy effective. The Carretera Marginal de la Selva is not simply a road but a vast complex of feeder roads, agricultural extension, land development, drainage and irrigation, marketing structures, land tenure systems, and the like. Without these "ancillary" investments, it is not likely that the exciting prospect of developing the eastern slope of the Andes can be achieved. Thus, the cost of the Carretera Marginal is not just the highway itself.

The fourth problem involves the often noted scarcity of projects.[6] Investment planning requires the choice among alternatives. Thus if there are no alternatives, there is no point to planning, though there always does exist the very important choice between doing something and nothing. But what are the alternatives? Are they not all the possible transport modes and the combinations of modes? Are they not, indeed, all the other relevant nontransport investments? In Peru, there is the choice between massive irrigation of the coastal desert as against the eastern slope highway. In Bolivia, there is the Oriente for possible development with transport oriented toward the Atlantic via Brazil or via the Parana River system through the River Plate estuary instead of highways in the Altiplano. But the point is that each alternative investment

must take the form of a project, worked out in detail by engineers, before it can be considered. And it is here that the
shortage of projects arises. Moreover, some projects will be
social in nature--public health, education, and the like--for
which planning and project development have yet to be developed
to a level of sophistication which will permit a proper comparison.

Fifth for consideration is the time profile of the development
process and of the projects' benefits and costs. If the pace of
development is very fast, as in Venezuela, then building highways
to very high standards is good economy since the rate of traffic
increase will begin to catch up with capacity well within the normal
financing period. By contrast, as with the Pan American Highway,
passing through Central America, opportunities for "staged construction" have not been and should not be overlooked. This means
that capacity is being increased by small increments over time as
the actual traffic counts build up. Moreover, though it is true
that a dollar spent today is worth more than a dollar spent ten
years from now, this fact alone ought not to be allowed to play a
preponderant role in investment decisions. It may also be true,
given the expected pace of development and the resultant changes
in the structure of the economy, that kinds of capacity not now
thought to be economic may become bottlenecks. For example,
the fast increase in the amount of passengers and freight moving
by highway through Peru, especially in and out of Lima, has
brought great pressure to bear on storage and terminal space in
the city well ahead of pressure on the carrying capacity of the highways themselves. In short, there is need for some understanding
of the maintenance cost profile, the likely pattern of use over time
as well as of the revenue or benefit pattern. This is, of course,
difficult, but the failure to take these matters into account may
well lead to supplying far too much or too little transport to accomplish the desired result.

Lastly, cost estimates even in advanced nations are subject to
wide margins of error. Moreover, these errors are seldom on
the low side. There is good reason, therefore, for the investment
plan to contain some recognition of this element of uncertainty by
indicating "confidence limits" for the cost estimates. What is the
range within which the costs are most likely to fall? This requires
a comparison of the experience of other planners and contractors
in similar situations elsewhere in the underdeveloped world.

THE PROCESS OF
TRANSPORT INVESTMENT PLANNING

A treatise on transport investment planning cannot contribute
much to the essential question in any form of planning. That
question is: What are the national goals? These the transport
investments are intended to permit the attainment of. If we
assume that the goals exist or have been expressed in some form,
then we have the context in which meaningful planning can take
place. Typically, in economic development terms at least these
goals involve not only increasing the level of domestic production
but also as widespread as possible a distribution of this production, both in the social and geographic sense. If this is the case,
then the first step in transport investment planning is a diagnosis
and forecast of the national economy.

What is sought in this diagnosis and forecast is both an understanding of the current structure of the economy and of its problems and a projection, based on a series of policy and investment
assumptions, regarding the paths of development of the national
economy. The simplest assumption regarding transport is that
increases in output and population depend on the provision of
transport capacity. Figures for the Soviet Union suggest that
during the period 1928-1950, for every 10% increase in total output, there was a 16% increase in traffic. In Asia, Owen has found
that over recent decades while domestic product increased from
2% to 5%, rail and road traffic increases ranged from about 6%
(the Philippines) to nearly 20% in Thailand. What seems to be
clear is that transport demand increases as domestic production
increases and generally at a rate faster than that of the domestic
product. The diagnosis and forecast should work out some of the
elements of such a projection.

In some cases, such as those involving demand rather than supply
strategies, the projections will be relatively simple. They will
turn out to be a form of demand analysis of the familiar varieties.
The techniques involved will work out simple or multiple re-
gression relations among such variables as income, population,
freight and passenger traffic indexes, and the like. If at the
same time account can be taken of the increasing productivity
of the available and emerging transport technology, a reasonably
accurate projection of demand and thus of transport requirements
can be worked out.

To be sure, the likelihood that such an analysis can be per-
formed in many Latin American nations, given the dramatic
effect of economic development upon the structure of their
economies is not as great as in more advanced nations. Rather
more care will have to go into the diagnosis and forecast, though
simpler analytic tools will be used. The translation of the general forecast into specific projects is much more difficult in Latin
America than in Western Europe and the United States and Canada. But this is the next step in the process of transport investment planning.

The diagnosis and forecast against the background of the stated
national objectives give the context within which the choice among
potential transport projects can proceed. But the assumption that
a large number of projects will be available for consideration is
likely to be a wrong one. As noted above, observers of the Latin
American scene have commented at length on the lack of projects
and have shown how this lack has tended to make inoperative the
planning process. They have made clear the need for the con-
tinual promotion of new project creation, by all the relevant
government agencies as well as the international agencies. It
turns out that few administrative bureaucracies are so organized
that they can devote their time and personnel resources to a far
enough look down the possible development paths to be in a position to create the range of projects necessary to permit that
pace of development. Moreover, planning agencies themselves
by the nature of their responsibilities and staff limitation are not
usually in a position to create new projects. Because public
works agencies are most likely to have a project orientation,
rather more transport projects will be available than perhaps
ought to be considered when the national goal and priorities are
carefully considered. But even in public works agencies, there
will not be as many projects as might be expected largely because
so much of the effort will necessarily be directed at completion of
work in hand.

The point is that the vital step from diagnosis and forecast to
project creation and analysis is not by any means an easy one.
Once again the advantage will lie with those nations where the
problem of transport investment is largely a matter of demand
rather than supply strategies. And it is these nations which are
already the more advanced and less likely to "need" assistance
in this respect. There is reason, therefore, for much more

emphasis on the part of the Agency for International Development (U.S.), the various associated agencies of the Bank for Reconstruction and Development, and the Inter-American Development Bank in the area of project development. This might take the form of studies of new applications of existing, as well as of newer, technologies. It certainly must take the form of creating an awareness of the role of the project in the achievement of stated ends.

The crucial step in the planning process is the evaluation and selection among projects. It almost goes without saying that the development process, by its nature which is essentially dynamic, takes the form of a continuous series of investment decisions. These decisions involve the selection among projects at various stages of elaboration, at various levels of sophistication and technical antecedents, as well as levels of engineering excellence. Obviously, the selection process and thus the development process will be more rational and capable of achieving stated ends, the more the decisions are based on a wide range of well-studied projects.

Though projects are essential for this selection process, it does not follow that because a nation possesses well-presented projects, all will or indeed that any of these will contribute to economic development. Care therefore must be taken to insure that the selection process is not just an internal evaluation of the individual projects. The selection criteria must be those which measure the likelihood of economic development and the degree and amount of such development to be obtained. Thus to have established that the Tejerias-Valencia autopista would yield a relatively high benefit over cost would not have been a sufficient reason for the planning authorities in Venezuela to approve its construction. In part, as the case study shows, the benefits were high because this was a part of a demand strategy. The essential question, even with the relatively large public works budgets possessed by Venezuelan authorities, ought to have been, does this proposed autopista advance the pace of economic development by increasing the national income. For example, does it provide such an increase by a greater amount than could be provided by some alternative project? There existed the possibility that this autopista was merely replacing an existing transport investment through a corridor already well developed where reductions in transport cost could be obtained (contributing thereby to the large net benefits) but with little increase in total production.

Needing some underlining is the requirement that selection criteria be development criteria rather than the traditional revenue or cost criteria.   To put the matter differently, care can well be exercised to insure that the project horizon and the decision context be national rather than local or agency oriented. That is to say, the transport or public works agency alone ought not to set the selection criteria.

ECUADOR: EXAMPLE
OF TRANSPORTATION PLANNING

Ecuador is one of the least developed of the nations on the South American continent.   With a current (middle 1960's) per capita income in the range between $200 and $225 and a growth rate about 2. 7% in per capita domestic production (1950 to middle 1960's), Ecuador has been growing relatively fast.   Nonetheless, successive governments of the nation have found it necessary to increase the pace of development.   The predominant economic characteristic of Ecuador has been the side-by-side growth of two quite distinct regions, one on the coast largely centered on the Guayas River Basin and the other in the valleys and plateaus of the high Andes, the "sierra."   Growth in these two regions has been quite unequal, with most of the recent advance occurring in the region from Guayaquil north into the ever-expanding agricultural frontier.

There are two basic objectives in recent national economic planning in Ecuador: (1) to step up the rate of growth in the export-oriented coastal provinces; and (2) to encourage the spread of that growth into the sierra.   The Ten Year Plan adopted for the years 1964-73 seeks to transform the social structure of the country so that more Ecuadorians will share in the benefits derived from foreign trade.   This transformation will take place through major land reform and colonization, largely on the coast, through community development both in the newer and older areas of settlement, improved transportation, administrative reform, increased incentives for private enterprise participation in the development process, widened educational opportunities especially directed toward the export sector, and a more effective role for the national government.

Presupposing a continuation of at least the same level of external support as over the previous ten years and no deterioration in the terms of trade for export crops, the Ecuador Plan envisages an even heavier dependence on exports than previously. The planners anticipate that tax resources and other government revenues from traditional sources will not be sufficient to finance the plan and that as a consequence the central government's role in the economy will tend to decline during the period so that "the nature and rhythm of development (in Ecuador) are going to depend more than ever on the possibility of obtaining an increase in exports."

The export forecasts call for an average annual rate of increase of 4.8% over the period. By 1968, it was anticipated that the traditional exports (bananas, coffee, rice, etc.) would represent some 81.6% of the total shipments and by 1973, some 75.7% so that "new" exports would be playing a more and more important role. Some of these exports would be elaborated and manufactured goods, as much as 17% by 1973. Import substitution, taking the form of more domestic production, would rise from 642 million sucres in 1968 to 867 million sucres by 1973.

To obtain this gain in export income and to bring about the planning social transformation, the basic infrastructure investment would be the expansion of the transport network, expecially on the coast. The order of priority of investments was set as follows:

1. Transport
2. Energy, water control, and irrigation
3. Agricultural bottlenecks
4. Import substitution and import capacity

Despite an enormous effort made since 1947, large areas of Ecuador were without access to markets because of a lack of transport. This was the major obstacle to economic growth seen by the National Planning Board. Thus the Plan provides for 1,050 kilometers of new highways and the improvement of 2,300 kms of existing highways during the first five years. This would largely be the completion of the highway network on the coast with practically no large projects.

During the second five years, 1969-73, the highway construction

was to be more disperse, a good share of it in the sierra. But
all highway planning "must be designed to cut freight costs as
much as possible." The criterion to be used was the ratio of
freight cost reduction to units of highway expenditures. Thus
the essence of the transport plan was to concentrate on those
zones where growth had already begun and which had a good
basic infrastructure or in those areas not far distant where the
possibility of export crop production was high. During the second five years, the purpose of highway construction would shift
to one of increasing the number of poles of growth so that self-
sustaining development could be induced all over the nation.

In effect, the Ecuador plan calls for the full development of
resources of Guayas River Basin.[8] This 33,640 square kilometer watershed of the Guayas River consists of a broad north-
south trending basin whose extensive southern flood plain merges
with an undulating and partially dissected landscape in the upper
river basin. The Guayas Basin is enclosed by the Steep Cordill-
era of the Andes to the east and lower ranges to the north and
west. This is the largest river valley on the Pacific Coast of
South America. The Guayas Basin probably has as great a diversity of climate conditions as can be found in any comparable
area in the Western Hemisphere. This extreme diversity is
due to the influence of the Andes and the ocean currents flowing
north along the coast from Antarctica. It differs sharply from
similar latitudes elsewhere in the tropics (between $0^{\circ}15'$ and
$2^{\circ}25'$ south latitude and $78^{\circ}40'$ and $80^{\circ}30'$ west longitude). The
Humboldt Current cools the southwest winds that penetrate the
Basin which, in addition to lowering the temperature, cause
cloudy conditions well into the interior. Precipitation taking
the form of snow in the highest elevations is heaviest during the
rainy season occurring from January to March. The actual a-
mount of rainfall varies greatly from a little south and west of
Guayaquil to upwards of 3,000 millimeters annually due east of
the city in the Andean foothills and to the north around Santo
Domingo de los Colorados.

The Guayas Basin is now the major supplier of bananas to world
markets. Its other export products exert little influence on
world suppliers but they and bananas are in direct competition
with produce from more favorably situated countries and face a
constant threat of substitution from alternative sources. Faced
with actual and potential competition from countries with low

world prices for primary produce, Ecuador planners must find
ways to continue to lower export costs. It is in this context
that the plan calls for extending and improving the existing inadequate highway network in the Guayas Basin. The road to be
constructed or improved under the plan, in addition to its
beneficial effects on exports prices, will also contribute to the
government's wider objectives of economic and administrative
integration of the country; of generally increasing and improving
output, quality and productivity in agriculture and industry; of
opening up new areas for colonization; of employing surplus
labor; of reducing transport costs to motor vehicle operators
and so economizing in scarce foreign exchange; of reducing
transport charges and travel times for road users thus inducing
economies in the use of capital tied up in inventories by a quicker
turnover of goods and generally widening the economic and social
horizons of the people of Ecuador.

Of the many individual highway projects proposed in the Ten
Year Plan, two are examined carefully in what follows with a
view to spelling out the selection criteria used. It should be
noticed, however, that by specifying the region to be developed,
as well as the reasons for this emphasis, the National Planning
Board of Ecuador had in effect limited the range of available projects. The following projects were from that range. They were
independent projects. Though they both serve the Guayas Basin,
either could be completed without direct effect on the region
served by the other or both if funds were adequate. The data to
support these choices were taken from reports both by the National Planning Board and the International Bank for Reconstruction and Development. [9]

The first of these is the Santo Domingo-Esmeraldas highway,
running from the northern part of the Guayas Basin into Esmeraldas province which encompasses the next river basin to the
north and west. Thus it links a new colonization area which has
been turning rapidly into one of the more prosperous regions of
the nation with a more tropical region in which is located Ecuador's third largest bananas shipment port.

The second is the Quevedo-Babahoyo-Duran highway, which con-
tributes a part of a future eastern trunk network in the Guayas
Basin. It runs north and south some fifteen to thirty-five kilometers east of the foothills of the Andes. It passes through a
region largely served by waterways, the Vinces and the Baba-

hoyo rivers and their tributaries. Products of the region include rice, bananas, cacao, coffee, sugar, fruits, cotton, and
timber. Grazing predominates in the eastern portion of the region. Small but potentially important sugar-and rice-processing
plants had been established in the region. The project will connect already existing stretches of highway and link them to the
port of Guayaquil at Duran (Alfaro).

The upgrading of Santo Domingo-Esmeraldas Road to a paved
all-weather highway should reduce the losses of produce through
bruising and rotting when transport is interrupted or delayed by
bad weather. It is also estimated that, at present, perhaps one-
quarter of the potential harvest of bananas is left unpicked on
the trees because of the lack of reliable transportation. The
assurance of regular produce evacuation and lower transportation costs offered by the project road may induce farmers
to offer for sale some of the produce which is now wasted. Reliable communications between the port and the planations will
make the scheduling of cutting, transport and ship-loading operations more efficient and thus economize on the use of capital
in local storage facilities. The better quality of banana, cheaper
production cost, and lower transportation cost will assist Ecuador in maintaining its position in the competitive world market.

The government of Ecuador forecasts that banana exports
through Esmeraldas will not increase substantially until after
the project road improvement is completed in 1967, and may
then rise to about 6.0 million stems by 1971. The government's
consultants expect that improvement to the road itself will increase the net output of agriculture from an area extending an
average of 2 km on each side. Their estimates have been checked
and appear reasonable on the basis of recent similar experiences
in Ecuador. The consultants also forecast modest increases in
traffic volumes after the opening of the road, starting at about
5% per annum and falling to less than 3-1/2% per annum after
ten years, when the traffic volume would be about 600 vehicles
per day.

The savings in vehicle operating costs for this growing traffic
are alone sufficient to provide a return of about 11%-12% on the
total investment in the road over its assumed useful economic
life. Supplemental agricultural benefits from the immediate
zone of influence contribute further to the economic justification.

The Quevedo-Babahoyo-Duran highway will provide improved facilities for the internal distribution of the products of the area and stimulate new developments in agriculture for both local and export markets. Substantial sections of road at the ends are already open to traffic and carry daily volumes up to 270 vehicles. At the opening of the through road in 1967, traffic is forecast to rise to about 400 vehicles per day on the existing road sections and 250 vehicles on new sections. Modest increases will result in daily traffic volumes in 1977 of about 670 vehicles and 410 vehicles, respectively, on the two main sections, Babahoyo-Duran and Quevedo-Babahoyo.

The future benefits expected to be derived from lower motor vehicle operating costs on the existing Babahoyo-Duran section of the road are estimated to provide a return of about 18% - 20% on the total investment in that section over its assumed useful economic life. The remaining section of road is justified as an essential link in the trunk road network, and also from consideration of the agricultural potential of the region traversed.

A brief summary is given below of the method used to estimate the benefits which accrue to the national economy from savings in vehicle operating costs when an existing road or track is improved or when a new and better transportation route is developed between two locations. The Santo Domingo-Esmeraldas road is used to illustrate the principles involved.

An analysis by the consulting engineers, based upon actual trucking and passenger car operations, gave the following costs of vehicle operation per km on roads in different physical conditions; the costs include vehicle depreciation, repairs, fuel, lubrication, tires, and drivers' salary for commercial vehicles:

Vehicle	Paved	Improved Unpaved	Unimproved
Heavy Truck	2.61	3.71	4.61 Sucres/km
Light Truck & Bus	2.05	2.60	3.05 Sucres/km
Passenger Car & Jeep	1.50	1.87	2.17 Sucres/km

The composition of present traffic on the unimproved Santo Domingo-Esmeraldas road results in a weighted average vehicle operating cost of about S/ 3.34 per km.

After improvement and paving of the road, and assuming no
material change in traffic composition, the weighted average
operating cost would reduce to about S/ 2.11 per km, effect-
ing a saving of S/ 1.23 per vehicle km, or about 36% of the
former cost.

Traffic projections were obtained as follows:

Normal Traffic Growth (on unimproved highway)

"Normal traffic growth" is that which would take place in any
case with a road maintained only in its present condition. The
average 1960 traffic volume on the unimproved Santo Domingo
road was 200 vehicles per day. Normal growth is assumed to be
an absolute annual increment equal to 5% of 1960 traffic, or 10
vehicles per day. Projections on this basis to 1982 are given
below:

	Actual	Projected			
	1960	1967	1972	1977	1982
ADT*	200	270	320	370	420
Annual Growth Per Cent	5	3.7	3.1	2.7	2.4

* Average Daily Traffic

Upon completion of a highway improvement (or construction of
a new highway) traffic will be induced because of the immediate
attractiveness of the improved (or new) facility. "Diverted"
(or attracted) traffic is that transferring from other routes or
other modes of transportation. "Generated" traffic consists
of new trips created by the existence of the improved (or new)
highway facility but not attributable to any resulting change in
land use, such as trips not previously made by any mode of transportation or those previously made by public transportation. It
is sometimes difficult to differentiate clearly between diverted
and generated traffic; both, however, usually develop within a
relatively short period after the opening of a new or improved
highway facility.

Diverted traffic over the improved Santo Domingo road is reasonably expected to consist of 70 vehicle trips per day of traffic transferring from the waterways, and a further 50 vehicle
trips because the port of Esmeraldas would then be more access-

ible than Guayaquil for some banana exporters, making a total of 120 diverted vehicles per day by or soon after completion of the works in 1967.

Traffic on any improved road will increase annually at a higher rate than normal growth due to the increased development of adjacent land, and output generally, over and above that which would have taken place normally with the road in its unimproved condition. This additional traffic is termed "development traffic."

Development traffic on the improved Santo Domingo road has been assessed at an extra 10 vehicles per day per annum after 1967, additional to the normal traffic growth of 10 vehicles per day per annum. The volume of development traffic is correlated to the amount of increased agricultural and other developmental activity.

A summary of the growth of normal, diverted and development traffic follows:

	1960	1967	1972	1977	1982
Normal	200	270	320	370	420
Diverted	-	120	120	120	120
Development	-	-	50	100	150
TOTAL	200	390	490	590	690
Per cent annual increment after improvement		5.1	4.1	3.4	2.9

The saving in vehicle operating cost over an improved facility is a measure of the longer life of vehicles and tires, reduced fuel consumption, quicker vehicle turnaround, etc. --in short, a measure of benefits to the vehicle fleet which accrue to the national economy.

In assessing such benefits, traffic over the improved facility must be considered in two different categories; (a) that due to normal growth; and (b) that diverted and developed. Normal traffic growth qualifies for the full amount of reduction in vehicle operating costs, while it is considered reasonable (in the absence of a better and more refined approach) to assess diverted and development traffic at about half that amount on the hypothesis that this type of traffic is induced proportionately to the amount of reduction in operating cost.

The equivalent traffic qualifying for full savings on the Santo
Domingo road, therefore, becomes:

	1967	1972	1977	1982
Normal	270	320	370	420
Additional	120	170	220	270
Total equivalent (veh/day)	330	405	480	555

A further reduction must be made since the traffic passing any
one point on the road does not necessarily travel its whole length.
The estimated average trip length for a vehicle on the Santo Domingo-Esmeraldas road has been taken by the consultants at 115
km compared with the total length of 174 km. Applying this cor-
rection to the above number of vehicles, the equivalent average
daily traffic running the whole road length and qualifying for full
savings is as follows:

	1967	1972	1977	1982
Equivalent ADT (veh/day)	220	270	320	370

For the year 1972, the savings in equivalent vehicle operating
costs would be: 270 (vehicles) x 365 (days) x 1.23 (S/ veh. km) x
174 (km) = 21.0 S / millions. Account must also be taken of the
annual difference in road maintenance costs resulting from the
new works. In the case of the Santo Domingo road no substantial
saving or increase in maintenance cost is envisaged.

Table I summarizes the basic data used in the calculations relating to capital costs, equivalent traffic volumes, weighted
savings, increased road maintenance costs, etc. Table II shows
the flow of benefits for the Santo Domingo road discounted first
at a rate of 8%, the average yield of government investment,
assumed to be as good a measure as any of opportunity cost of
public capital in Ecuador, and then at a rate (determined by trial
and error) such as will equate the value of the cumulative discounted benefits to the total capital investment over an assumed
20-year economic life for the improved road.

TABLE I

Summary of Basic Economic Data

Ecuador Highway Projects

(Vehicle Operating Cost Only)

Road	Road Length (km)	Trip Length (km)	Traffic Volumes (v.p.d.)				Weighted Veh. Op. 2 Savings (S/km)	Per Cent Reduction Veh. Op. Cost
			Actual 1960	Projected Equiv. ADT 1967	1977	1987		
1 Sto.Domingo-Esmeraldas	174	115	200	220	320	420	1.23	36
2 a) Quevedo-3 Babahoyo	139	90	-	230	410	590	-	-
b) Babahoyo-Duran	60	58	265	370	565	760	0.69	20

1 Average Daily Traffic corrected for assumed trip lengths and including half of diverted and development traffic.

2 Based upon traffic composition and vehicle operating costs over roads prior to and after construction/improvement; composition is assumed materially constant.

3 Traffic volumes are those estimated to divert from waterways plus development traffic; transportation savings cannot be determined since waterway transport costs are not known.

TABLE I, continued

Road	Previous Expenditure	Cost to Complete	Eng. Esc. and Conting.	Interest[5]	Total Capital Invested	Increased Annual Maint.	Period to Recover Investment @8% (years)	Approximate Internal rate of return 20 Year Amortization Per Cent
		-- sucres	million--					
1 Sto. Domingo-Esmeraldas	10.5	110	38.5	18	177	-	13	12
2 a) Quevedo-Babahoyo	51	80	28.3	13.2	172	2.2	Not possible to determine	
b) Babahoyo-Duran	-7	24	8.0	3.5	36	-	8	20[6]

5 Assumed 8% for half construction period.
6 These rates reduce by 1% or 2% if development traffic benefits are omitted.
7 Assumed already amortized by previous benefits.

TABLE II
Estimated Flow of Economic Benefits, Santo Domingo-Esmeraldas Road
(Vehicle Operating Savings Only)

Estimated Total Cost: 177 million sucres (see Table I)

During Year:	Equivalent ADT	Vehicle Operating Benefits*	Discounted at 8%	Discounted at 12%
1 (1967)	220	17.0	17.0	17.0
2		17.8	16.5	15.8
3		18.6	16.0	14.8
4		19.4	15.4	13.8
5		20.2	14.9	12.8
6 (1972)	270	21.0	14.3	11.9
7		21.8	13.8	11.0
8		22.6	13.2	10.2
9		23.4	12.7	9.4
10		24.2	12.1	8.7
11 (1977)	320	25.0	11.6	8.0
12		25.8	11.1	7.4
13		26.6	10.6	6.8
14		27.4	179.2	6.2
15		28.2		5.7
16 (1982)	370	29.0		5.2
17		29.8		4.8
18		30.6		4.4
19		31.4		4.0
20		32.2		3.7
21 (1987)	420	33.0		181.6

* The same as total benefits since in this example no saving or
  increase in highway maintenance cost is envisaged.

DEDUCTIONS:
a) Investment will be recovered in 13th year of operation at
    8% assumed interest rate.
b) Internal rate of return with assumed economic life of 20
    years: 12%.

AGRICULTURAL BENEFITS

It was conservatively assumed that there would be a narrow zone of influence 2 km wide on each side of those project roads traversing fertile agricultural lowlands. New lands eventually brought under cultivation as a direct result of the project works would amount to about 25% of this limited zone of influence, that is, would be equal to a cultivable area of 100 hectares per kilometer of road.

The areas estimated to be developed by the project highways are summarized below:

Road Ref.	Road	Length (km)	Along-side Road	Beyond Terminals	Total
			Area Developed (Hectares)		
1	Sto. Domingo-Esmeraldas	174	17,000	-	17,000
2	Quevedo-Duran	199	20,000	-	20,000

The estimate of the net annual value of agricultural production (after making provision for the farmers' own investment) was approximately S/ 2,000 per hectare for areas traversed by the project roads twenty years after their completion. The estimates are based upon typical net values per hectare, made at the time of the project study, of S/ 4,000 for bananas, S/ 2,000 for cacao, S/ 5,600 for palm oil, and S/ 725 for coffee.

The resultant value of the net increase in agricultural production after completion of the project roads in 1967 is given below:

Above Road Ref.	Area Developed (hectares)	1967	1972	1977	1982	1987
		Net Annual Increase, Agricultural Production (sucres million)				
1	17,000	nil	11.0	18.7	26.4	34.0
2	20,000	nil	13.0	22.0	31.0	40.0

COMPARISON OF BENEFITS WITH ROAD INVESTMENT

An agricultural development road usually constitutes only one element of a complex and integrated regional development scheme, and difficulties arise when attempting to assign portions of the estimated net agricultural benefits from the whole region to any one element such as the road itself.

These roads are primarily trunk highways connecting sizable community centers; increased agricultural production is incidental and has been assumed to develop, for the most part, spontaneously, since very little investment capital is required. However, some rough assessment has been made of the likely additional public investment required to realize the increased production in the limited service areas adjacent to the roads.

A general study by the Ecuadorian National Institute of Colonization in the Santo Domingo area has shown that a public capital requirement of S/ 65.8 million would be needed to develop 170,000 hectares, including the provision of feeder roads, schools, housing, social services, farm loans, etc. This represents an average public investment required of about S/ 400 per hectare (additional to any capital invested in major highways) if the estimated agricultural benefits from the region are to be realized.

The above figure, plus 50% for possible additional public costs and other contingencies, making a total of S/ 600 per hectare, has been applied to the limited areas assumed developed directly by the project roads. A comparison has then been made of the net values of agricultural production with the total public capital invested, including provision for highway maintenance. The results are summarized in Table III and indicate approximate rates of return on total capital from agricultural benefits alone of about 5% - 6%.

It is emphasized that the figures on the table only indicate the broad orders of magnitude of the economic benefits deriving from the agricultural influence of the project roads. The limited agricultural data available do not permit anything more than a rough estimation to be made.

The approximate values of the economic benefits resulting from savings in vehicle operating costs and from increased agricultural production have been assessed in the foregoing sections

TABLE III

Calculation of Net Annual Benefits from Highway
Investment in Santo Domingo (Ecuador)

Ref.	Road	Capital Invested in Road[1]	Additional Development Capital[2]	Total Capital Invested	Increased Annual Road Maintenance	Net Annual Benefits[3]			Approx. Rate of Return[4]
						1967	1977	1987	
1	Sto. Domingo-Esmeraldas	177	10	187	0	0	+18.7	+34.0	6%
2	Quevedo-Duran	208	12	220	2.2	-2.2	+19.8	+37.8	5%

(figures in S/million)

1 Including previous expenditures, engineering, escalation, contingencies, and interest during construction.
2 Developed area within zone of influence x S/ 600 per hectare.
3 Net annual value of increase in agricultural production less increased annual highway maintenance cost.
4 Discount rate to equate cumulative present values of net benefits to total capital investment.

and expressed independently as approximate rates of return
on the respective capital investments. When attempting to combine the two benefits, the following complications arise:

(a)   The vehicle operating benefits are related
       to public capital invested in the road alone,
       while the agricultural benefits are related
       to the public capital invested in a regional
       complex of which the road constitutes but
       one element;

(b)   There may be some duplication or double-
       counting of assessed benefits since develop-
       ment traffic exists by virtue of increased
       agricultural production, and reduced trans-
       portation costs have already been taken into
       account when expressing net values of pro-
       duction.

The following approach enables an approximate assessment of
the combined benefits to be made:

(a)   Since the project roads are the most impor-
       tant elements in the agricultural complexes
       under consideration, and since the major
       portion of public capital (here, about 95%) is
       invested in the roads, it is reasonable to
       assume that the major portion of the net agri-
       cultural benefits (say about 90%) may be cred-
       ited to the roads;

(b)   To avoid possible duplication, the above por-
       tion of net agricultural benefits should be com-
       bined with those vehicle operating benefits de-
       riving from normal and attracted traffic only,
       excluding development traffic.

On the above basis, taking the Santo Domingo-Esmeraldas road
as an example, the economic benefits accruing from different
sources have been combined and are expressed below as a return on capital invested in the road, making due allowance for
road maintenance costs. Vehicle operating benefits have been
broken down into components according to the nature of the

traffic benefiting in order to illustrate their relative contributions:

Vehicle Operating Benefits			Combined Vehicle Operating and Agricultural Benefits
Norm.	Norm. Div.	Norm. Div. Dev.	
(*) (1)	(2)	(3)	(4)
9%	11%	12%	17%

(*) (1) Normal traffic growth only
     (2) Normal growth, with Diverted traffic at half-weighting
     (3) Normal growth, with Diverted and Development traffic
         both at half-weighting
     (4) Traffic benefits from (2) combined with 90% net agricultural benefits

Summarizing, the savings in vehicle operating costs from improving the Santo Domingo-Esmeraldas road are alone sufficient to provide a minimum return on total investment of about 9% from normal traffic growth, and a probable return of about 11%-12% including likely additional traffic, over the useful economic life of the road. Supplemental agricultural benefits, which are less certain and more difficult to measure, may raise this rate of return to about 17%.

SUMMARY AND CONCLUSIONS

Ideally, transport planners should be able to place their project proposals in the context of national planning. These plans which are themselves the presentation of the political purposes of electorate or of the relevant national administration provide the setting for the selection of transport investment strategies. But the ideal, of course, is not always attainable. Yet, it may be well to proceed as if a plan did exist, spelling out what might have been the elements of such a plan. Then some concept of the range of alternative projects becomes possible of development. And this concept will permit a more effective evaluation of any project proposal. At the very least, transport planners because they possess certain advantages over planners in other sectors of the economy must not overplay these advantages to the possible detriment of the national economy. Surely it is never enough to embark on a transport project because "we know how to build it."

Notes to Chapter 5

[1] Cf. Wilfred Owen, Strategy for Mobility (Washington,
D. C. : The Brookings Institution, 1964), esp. Chapter VII.
This is an excellent presentation of the role of transport
in economic development.

[2] Cf. "General Problems in Transportation in Latin
America, " Doc 18-A (Washington, D. C. : Pan American Union,
3 July, 1964).

[3] Wolfgang Friedmann, Raymond Mikesell, and George
Kalmanoff, "The Atlantic Railway, " in Public International De-
velopment Financing in Colombia (New York: Department of
International Legal Research, June, 1963).

[4] Plan General de Desarrollo Economico, (1964-1973), Libros I y I
(Quito, Ecuador: Junta Nacional de Planificacion, 1963).

[5] Clell G. Harral, Preparation and Appraisal of Transport
Projects (Washington, D. C. : The Brookings Institution, October,
1965) (Mimeographed.)

[6] Cf. Discusiones sobre Planificacion, Informe de un
seminario (Mexico: Siglo XXI, Editores, SA; 1966), esp.
Capitulo IV.

[7] Cf. Owen, op. cit. , Chapter III.

[8] Cf. Survey for the Development of the Guayas River Basin
of Ecuador (Washington, D. C. : Pan American Union, 1964).

[9] Much of the specific detail presented in the following pages
is taken from lecture notes for Economic Development Seminars
at the International Bank for Reconstruction and Development. The
primary sources are varied, coming from consultants' reports
and from the Junta Nacional de Planificacion del Ecuador. For
more detail, see the Plan General de Desarrollo Economico,
(1964-1973), (Quito, Ecuador: Junta Nacional de Planificacion, 1963).

APPENDIXES

MEASUREMENT OF BENEFITS FROM
TRANSPORT INVESTMENTS

Just how to measure the benefits[1] which accrue from a transport project has persistently been a problem. And it is all the more a problem in the context of underdevelopment. In this appendix, let us take a careful analytical look at the various suggested measures of these benefits, keeping in mind that in each of the case studies presented, we had an example of one or more such measures. The study of the Colombian freight transport system was, in fact, a critical analysis of a widely favored benefit measure, namely the extent to which there is integration within transport modes. It was argued that if this benefit measure is to be used, a more encompassing concept of transport modes must be applied, one which regards all transport as part of the means used by a nation to solve its problems of moving the goods it needs.

In the Venezuelan highway case, we tried to apply three kinds of measures, a limited user-benefit measure, a more general gain in regional income measure and finally an indicator of the effect on the pace of national economic development. In the Carretera Marginal study, we took a very long look down the potential development paths and sought to see what the benefits would be at some horizon, that horizon being the point in time when the road and all the ancillary works were in place. But in each case, we took account both of the nature of the data available and of the decision to be made in the selection of the benefit measure to be used. That is to say, there was a good deal of an "ad hoc" approach to the matter. Can more be said than this?

As observed, part of the problem the analyst faces arises from the fact of underdevelopment. What is meant by underdevelopment? If we assume that underdevelopment means the underemployment of existing resources including technical know how, then there is an implication that if a transport project could bring the nation to a fuller use of its resources, the increase in aggregate demand and income which resulted would be the measure of the benefit. If it is land that is underemployed, then the measurement becomes quite a bit easier. What a transport facility does, then, is to overcome those barriers, usually

179

geographic,to a fuller utilization of the potential land resources.
Obviously, land supplies could also be increased through improved irrigation, control of health hazards, offsetting of climatic discomfort, and the like. Generally, though, these and
similar projects are ancillary to the transport facilities.

In an undeveloped country, not only is the level of domestic
product lower than it would be if all resources were in full use,
but the productivity of all the factor of production is less than
would be obtained under fuller employment. Some of the labor
and capital now being employed is in use on land where the marginal product is quite low. A shift of this labor and capital to
other and better land would lead to a higher marginal product
and thus to an increase in the total domestic product.

Suppose we consider the case, examined in some detail by
Hirsch,[2] in which El Salvador increased the land available for
cotton production through the building of the Pacific Litoral
Highway. Prior to the highway, though there was no evidence
that Salvadorean cotton production was at its possible maximum, there was evidence that the existing farms were using
land the fertility of which was lower than that of undeveloped
land along the coast. With the highway in place, there was a
relatively rapid increase in the conversion of new lands to
cotton production. Along with this conversion, and more than
likely a cause of it, was the increase in cotton exports. Thus,
the productivity of the new lands was increased, and this increase in productivity showed up in more money per unit of
effort and of land as well as in increased exports all of which
would be counted as increases in the national income.

The increase in national income though has other effects
worth examining. If there is an increase in real per capita income as a consequence, then if Engel's Law is operative,[3] the
demand for consumer goods will behave in the following manner.
The old line staples will have a less than proportional increase
in sales as "newer" consumer items will have grown faster
than income in sales and purchases. This means a widening of
the consumer budget. But it also means that newer industries
(and/or new imports) will benefit from the effect of the transport facility. This effect may not be obvious and may be harder
to trace than the direct benefits, but it is clearly not to be overlooked.

Moreover, if consumer prices fall or, what is the same thing, incomes rise faster than consumer prices, then we may have a consumer's surplus effect to examine. To be sure, there could have been a direct consumer's surplus effect for the users of the new facility when they found the transport costs lower than those they had been accustomed to pay. The difference between what they could have been induced to pay to transport their goods and what they now pay is such a surplus. But it is not this surplus that is of importance. Rather it is the general consumer's surplus which arises from the general fall in consumer prices. Now consumers generally are able to pay less than they could have been induced to pay, as witnessed by what they did pay in the prehighway case.

It is not clear that national income accounting will be able to pick up this consumer's surplus measure of benefit, at least at first. But, this surplus and the operation of Engel's Law are closely related since it is likely that any real increase in income-- such as that arising from being able to pay staples at lower prices--will be spread over other commodities, thus increasing the demand for them. Sooner or later, the consumer's surplus benefit will show up in national income.

All of this seems to lead to a conclusion that we can safely use national income measures to attain relatively complete measures of benefit. But let us see more directly how various measures are related. One measure left out in what follows is that of profit. Private or agency profitability measures (used by Ministries of Public Works, for example) will not in general be comparable to national income because profitability tends to exclude not only the intangible social benefits to classes and economic groups beyond the immediate range of the transport project's influence but also the external economies (or secondary repercussions) likely to be derived from that project. Yet if we make profits equivalent to cost savings or shippers' savings, we can see what relationship there is between national income and agency private profits, as well as local gains. That is the purpose of the following table, taken from Harral.

Measure A is national income. Measures B, C, and D, whose components represent other commonly used measures of benefits, are defined so that they are conceptually equivalent to each other and to the increase in national income, measure A.

TABLE A-I[4]
Comparison of National Income Measure and Other
Measures of Benefits of Transport Improvements

All measures are equivalent: Measure A = Measure B =
Measure C = Measure D, and each Measure is composed of
one or more separate elements numbers (A), (B. 1), (B. 2), etc.

Measure A National Income Approach	(A) Increase in national income due to investment in transport and complementary activities.

Measure B Cost Savings Approach	(B. 1) Transport cost savings on present traffic and traffic which would develop without transport improvement

plus

Increase or decrease in
economic efficiency of employed resources due to increase of feasible plant
scale and improved tech-
nologies:
(B. 2) Near the transport facility,
(B. 3) and Elsewhere in the economy.

plus

Employment of formerly idle
resources in areas:
(B. 4) Adjacent to transport facility,
(B. 5) and Elsewhere in the economy.

Measure C	(C. 1) Increased profits to trans- port carriers

plus

182

(C. 2) Savings to shippers located near the transport
facility

plus

(C. 3) Savings to shippers located elsewhere but who
ship over the given facility

(The sum of elements (C. 1) + (C. 2) + (C. 3) = element
(B. 1).)

plus

(B. 2), (B. 3), (B. 4), and
(B. 5) as above

Measure D
Rents or Land
Value Approach

(D. 1) Element (C. 1) as above

plus

(D. 2) Increase in income accruing
to owners of land and other
realty near the transport
facility as rents

(Element (D. 2) equals the decapitalized increase in value of
land and other realty near the facility.)

(Element (D. 2) also equals the sum of elements (C. 2) + (B. 2).)

plus

(C. 3), (B. 3), (B. 4), and
(B. 5) as above.

Comparison of these measures in this format helps to make
clear why partial measures such as transport cost savings,
shippers savings, profits and land value changes can so easily
be misrepresented in estimates of the benefits of transport investments. These measures may either ignore various effects,
such as elements (B. 3), (B. 4), and (B. 5) and sometimes (B. 2)
and therefore tend to understate the actual increase in national
income. Or they may add together two or more elements,
which reflect one and the same benefit, and thus overstate the
increase in income. For example, it has not been unusual to
observe either cost savings (B. 1) or (C. 2) added to (D. 2), the
increase in land rents which reflect the reduction in transport
costs. To use such a measure represents double counting of
actual benefits.

Transport cost savings have been the most commonly applied
measure of benefits since they are relatively easy to estimate.
The cost savings usually consist of the expected reduction in
operating and maintenance costs resulting from the investment,
which are weighed against the estimated capital costs of the
project. If reliable cost data are available, cost savings are
an acceptable measure of the benefits of a transport investment,
where little change in land use, production, and traffic patterns
are expected.

Cost savings are inappropriate as the measure of benefits
where major changes in land use, production, and traffic
patterns are expected because this measure excludes the increase in efficiency of presently employed resources and new
employment of formerly idle resources in the area most directly
served by the transport facility.

The greater the amount of the saving through reduced charges
to shippers and the greater their elasticity of supply, the greater will be the response of the economy in increased output, employment, and income. However, if all the transport cost reductions serve only to increase the carriers' profits and there
are no reductions in the rates charged shippers, the beneficial
effect of the investment on the economy may be minimal. But
if transport operators are enterprising in using their increased
profits and finance new equipment, improved service, and other
productive investments from them, transport cost savings become the source of sizable new investments.

The national income approach whatever other advantages it
may have permits the analyst to pick up most of the effects
of an investment.   The new investment induced by transport
cost savings as well as other complementary investments,
such as housing, fertilizers, storage facilities, and the like,
will be counted.   It is this last advantage which is of such importance that it appears to suggest exclusive use of this approach.
However, it is seldom indeed that data are available in the form
or to the extent necessary to permit its use.   For these practical reasons, there will probably continue to be rather more use
of partial and/or local criteria.   Therefore, the demonstration
in Table I that there is some equivalence among commonly used
approaches is of more than theoretical importance.

THE USE OF THE
NATIONAL INCOME APPROACH

The basic methodology involved in the use of the national income
approach is the development of two projections: one showing how
the national income would have increased in the absence of the
proposed transport investment and the other showing how much
higher the national income would be with the transport investment in place.   The difference between these two projections is
taken to be the benefit attributable to the transport project.   Typically, of course, it will not be national but rather regional or sec-
toral income that will be the proper measure.

If we can assume that enough data are available to permit us to
make several observations at distinct periods of time of the income in the region, then extrapolation from these observations requires some estimating of both the no-investment and postinvest-
ment growth rates.   Even more important, however, are some
accounting problems.   Suppose that we had the gross output of a
given region for any period of time; we should want then to deduct
all purchases of intermediate goods from outside the region, as
well as all wages, profits and interest payable to resources drawn
into use in the region from productive employment elsewhere in
the nation.   This is what Harral calls the "deductible costs method." Barbara Bergmann has proposed an alternate method which
would take the gross output, multiply it by the percentage of value
added in that region and subtract from it the wages, profits, and
interest payable to resources drawn into the region from productive
employment elsewhere.   This is the "percentage-value-added"
method.

What can be said about the application of the national income
approach is presented in Table II.

TABLE A-II

National Income Benefits Criterion: projected national income if transport and related investments are undertaken minus
projected national income if investments are not undertaken,
plus most specific description possible for any closely related
noneconomic benefits.

PROCEDURE

1.   Determination of the form which transport cost savings
      and service improvements take: estimation of service
      characteristics and unit costs of transport for all policy
      alternatives, including doing nothing to present system.

2.   Delineation of the economic region which will contain the
      major part of the repercussions of the proposed invest-
      ments on the location of agricultural, forestry, mining and
      industrial production, employment, and income.

3.   Projection of future agricultural, forestry, mining and
      industrial production, employment, and income, with
      geographic location specified for the smallest possible
      geographic unit.

4.   Valuation of predicted output at true opportunity values
      over time: In general, gross outputs should be valued
      at known or estimated wholesale prices, adhering to the
      following principles:

      a.   Outputs destined for export or for import sub-
            stitution should be valued at the opportunity
            cost of foreign exchange.

      b.   Future outputs for export or for import substitu-
            tion should be valued at the predicted future oppor-
            tunity cost of foreign exchange, taking into account
            any anticipated fluctuations in international prices.

TABLE A-II, continued

c. Changes in over-all domestic price levels should
be statistically eliminated by valuing future output for domestic consumption at prices constant
at initial level.

5. Netting-out intermediate purchases and shifts of productive
resources from other regions. For each economic sector
determine net income or value added in wages, interest,
and profits by either or both methods:

a. Deductible costs method:

Net sector income = gross output minus purchase of
intermediate goods minus wages,
profits, and interest of resources
shifted into the region from productive employment outside the
region.

b. Percentage-value-added-method:

Net sector income = (Gross output value) x (percentage-
value-added in this sector) minus
wages, profits, interests of resources shifted into the region from
productive employment outside the
region.

6. Increase in national income = sum of increases in net value
added for each sector. [6]

A CONSUMER'S SURPLUS
MEASURE OF BENEFITS

The neoclassical consumer's surplus was developed as a tool
to measure not only the relative changes in consumer economic
welfare as prices changed in the marketplace but also to indicate
the benefits derived from economic development. It is not surprising that many analysts have attempted to apply it to situations
involving transport investments. Under what conditions can this
measure of benefits be used? What are some of the problems implicit in its use? Let us examine some facts taken from a real
case to see what can be said.

Assume the following facts:[7] Prior to the building of the Cochabamba-Santa Cruz highway, a certain established pattern
of consumption characterized a particular zone. This pattern
of consumption depended upon the pattern and use of the productive resources of the zone as well as upon importation from
other zones. The real price structure--real in the sense that
it takes account of the labor cost--reflected the relative cost
pattern as well as the current--and possibly traditional--state
of demand. Now suppose that following the construction of the
highway, we find a different pattern of consumption, different
at least in that more of some commodities are being purchased
than before.

Had we prices to work with, we should quite probably attempt
to work out a measure of the consumer's surplus arising from
this change. The procedure followed would involve determining
the amounts purchased at the old prices and then the amounts purchased at the new prices. Thus in the example given this amounts
to 24,000 pesos. The reduction in price has brought a substantial
benefit to consumers. To the extent that this reduction can be
traced to the new road, it is a measure of the benefit of the
investment.

In measuring the consumer's surplus in this fashion, of course,
we have had to make some assumptions. One of the most obvious of these is that demand conditions before and after the in-
stallation of the highway were essentially the same. We have
also assumed that there was no income effect which had it
existed might have distributed some of the gains to other markets
(i.e., for other products than that for which our demand curve
is applicable). This means that with 24,000 pesos, we assume
that we have a measure of all of the benefit arising from the
change in the economic situation. Obviously, if any of the
benefit arising from the reduction in price led to an increase in
the purchase of other commodities and services, then our
consumer's surplus measure is less than complete as an
indication of the benefit.

In general, however, as long as we have the requisite price
information and no real reason to suppose a significant income

EXAMPLE 1

	Price (pesos)	Quantity (kgs)	Expenditures (pesos)
BEFORE ROAD	1.00	100,000	100,000
AFTER ROAD	0.80	140,000	112,000

CALCULATION OF RELATIVE CONSUMERS' SURPLUS

Quantity Before Road times Price Before Road	= 100,000 pesos
Quantity Before Road times Price After Road	= 80,000 pesos

$$SAVING_1 \qquad = 20,000 \text{ pesos}$$

Quantity After Road times Price Before Road	= 140,000 pesos
Quantity After Road times Price After Road	= 112,000 pesos

$$SAVING_2 \qquad = 28,000 \text{ pesos}$$

Difference Between $SAVING_2$ and $SAVING_1$ $\qquad$ = 8,000 pesos

$$RELATIVE\ CONSUMERS'\ SURPLUS = SAVING_1 + 1/2 \times$$
$$(SAVING_2 - SAVING_1)$$
$$= 20,000 \times 1/2\ (8,000)$$
$$= 24,000 \text{ pesos}$$

effect, this is a good measure. There are, nonetheless, three
difficulties likely to arise in less-developed countries with such
a measure. The first of these is that inflation tends to mar the
clarity of the price picture. While there is no need in such
cases as these to inquire about the nature and cause of the inflation, its effect is such as to have prices higher in the after situation than in the before.

The second difficulty is that the less developed the country, the
more important is likely to be the income effect. [8] Incomes are
at or near subsistence and increases are quite probably going to
be used to widen and deepen the range of the consumer budget so
as to include items not thought obtainable before. As observed
above, this weakens the effectiveness of the consumer's surplus
as a measure of benefit.

The third difficulty is that the very effect of a new highway is
more than likely to change the demand function particularly
toward introducing new tastes as well as increasing incomes, if
not changing the form and quality of the goods and services
offered in the market. In addition, there is always the possibility that the prices of staples might not change at all--in the
absence of inflation. The existence of a traditional price for
rice, for example, may prevent any reduction in the price. This
is all the more true if the price reflects traditional producer and
retailer margins. Moreover, any producer of the staple may regard a potential reduction in price as having too great an income
effect to run the risk that he could recover from a substitution
effect. Then again, he might not be in a position to increase his
own production.

The consumer's surplus is appropriate, it turns out, only to a
state of economic development when consumers' budgets have
come to be quite large in content and when the problem of subsistence is no longer germane. But when the margin between
income and consumption is narrow as must be the case for many
persons--if not the vast majority--in the underdeveloped world,
it is certainly questionable whether it is applicable.

All these factors tend to make the consumer's surplus less applicable to our problem than we had hoped. But all is by no means
lost. We have been talking about a rather special measure of the
consumer's surplus, one made popular by Alfred Marshall among
others. [9] But it is not the only such measure available. Marshall's

concept like many similar tools of analysis developed by neoclassical economists is relative.   There always was the "absolute" consumer's surplus, in the Hicksian sense. [10]

A relative surplus arises out of the comparison of two possible price-quantity combinations of a single demand function.
The surplus is the difference between what is and what might
have been had a different price-quantity combination been obtained.   An absolute surplus is the difference between the level
of consumer income and the cost of obtaining that level.   In this
case, the cost of living is the relevant concept and may be
thought to be measured by the necessary subsistence required to
keep a consumer alive.   Now let us see how an absolute consumer's surplus can be calculated.

We know the following things about the before and after situation.   We know the consumption patterns in both situations.   We
have had an inflation so that the price index has risen substantially between the period of the planning of the road and its ter-
mination.   Perhaps largely as a consequence the cost of trans-
port--tires, gasoline, repairs, and maintenance--has gone up.
We also know that there has been a significant increase in the
traffic entering the Oriente over the highway and that many
more of traditional commodities are entering along with some
new commodities not previously available.

The price index measures the changes in the cost of a "market
basket" of commodities and services.   We might attempt to
work out the "real"change in consumer income in the zone by
using the index to deflate a wage series.   But when this is done,
to our surprise we get an apparent reduction in "real" income.

But there is evidence of increased sales, as well as increased
movement of traffic and a wider range of goods in the market.
Moreover, we do know that the new pattern of consumption includes not only more of the traditional goods but also some of
the goods and services not previously available.   On the face of
it, there is a paradox.   Real income as measured by a deflated
wage series would appear to have declined while real income as
measured by what is actually purchased would seem to have increased.

We can see that the relative consumer's surplus would not be
of help here.   Why?   Suppose, for example, that the price of

rice had risen as between the before and after situations, from
1 peso to 1.50 pesos.   This should have led to a reduction in
consumption on the assumption that nothing else had changed,
say to 80,000 kgs.; and using the previous example, since the
consumers now pay 1.50 pesos and buy 80,000 kgs., rather
than 100,000 kgs. at 1 peso, they have lost approximately
37,000 pesos in consumer's surplus.

Our survey of consumption habits after the construction of the
highway reveals, however, that consumers in the zone now buy
140,000 kgs. at the new price of 1.50 pesos.   Under the relative surplus mode of reasoning, we should now measure the
total expenditure at 1.50 pesos and compare it with what would
have been spent had the price remained at 1.00 pesos.   This
"loss" in consumers' surplus now mounts to approximately
70,000 pesos.

However, it is apparent that the increase of 40,000 kgs. of
rice is an improvement over the before situation.   To determine the absolute surplus gain, we return to the before market.
We work out the proportion rice represented of total consumption.   Suppose that this had been 33-1/3% of the consumer budget prior to the construction of the highway.   In addition to the
100,000 pesos spent on rice in the old situation, some 200,000
pesos were being spent on other things, making a total expenditure of 300,000 pesos, at the old price level.

Now in the new situation, 140,000 kgs. of rice are being purchased at 1.50 pesos which totals 210,000 pesos.   If there
has been no change in the budget proportions, this implies a
new total expenditure of 630,000 pesos.   If we further assume
that all prices tended to move up about 50%, as indicated by the
price index and that we can convert all the other goods and
service in the budget into kg. equivalents, it would appear that
consumers are getting in the new situation 40,000 more kgs. of
rice and 80,000 more kg. of everything else.   The value of
this addition to real income at the new prices is 180,000 pesos.

However, our new market basket survey reveals that rice in
the new situation occupies only 25% of the consumer budget.
That gives us an indicated total expenditure of 840,000 pesos.
It also means some 220,000 more kgs. of everything else plus
40,000 more kgs. of rice, an addition to real income which at
the new prices in the new situation would be worth 390,000 pesos.

If we regard rice by itself as an index of the cost of living, then the indicated increase in consumers' surplus is 210,000 pesos. If, on the other hand, we add that rice plus housing and clothing represented the basic cost of living and that taken together this amounted to 75% of the consumers' budgets in the old situation but 66-2/3% in the new situation, this would give us an estimate of 205,000 pesos as the increase in consumers' surplus. The first approach assigns all benefits to changes in the price of rice. The second makes the more reasonable assumption that all the "cost of living" or subsistence items tended to share in the change in a way analogous to Engel's Law.

In addition to permitting us to say something meaningful about the benefits accruing to consumers from the construction of the highway, this measure has the advantage of permitting none of these benefits to escape our notice. The 40,000 additional kilograms of rice enabled us to trace other changes in the consumer budget and thus to give a value to these improvements.

An examination of the different possible measures of benefit does not itself settle all the issues. As observed in Chapter 5, a decision to undertake a particular transport project is part of an economic development strategy. Often when the benefit criteria are presented, the best context is that indicated in the following summary statement regarding the (Bolivian) Cochabamba-Santa Cruz highway: "If the road was necessary and desirable for economic developmental and political reasons, it has already proved worthwhile from the economic viewpoint."[11] But the analyst goes on to observe that "if we attempt to answer the larger questions raised by the 'Aswan Dam' strategy of Bolivian development, implied by large investments in transportation links to the lowlands, then it is clear that the most important part of the answer lies in those benefits which we have not attempted to estimate numerically."

To put the matter in a different light, any measure of benefit by itself cannot be used to determine whether any project is worthwhile. What such a measure does is to present the results of an economic analysis. If the issues of development were entirely economic ones, this presentation would prove to be weighty. But such is not always nor even usually the case. Perhaps, too, it needs to be pointed out that benefit measures do not indicate

EXAMPLE 2

	Price of Rice/kg	Quantity of Rice/kg	Expenditure on Rice/pesos	Rice as Share of Total Expenditures	Total Expenditures/pesos
Before Road	1.00	100,000	100,000	1/3	300,000
After Road	1.50	140,000	210,000	(a) 1/3 (b) 1/4	(a) 630,000 (b) 840,000

(a) assumes no change rice proportion of total expenditure
(b) records actual change in rice proportion of total expenditure

CALCULATION OF ABSOLUTE CONSUMER'S SURPLUS, RICE AS INDEX OF COST OF LIVING

No change in Rice Proportion of Total Expenditures, Before and After Road

Increase in Rice Expenditures   40,000 kgs
Increase in other Expenditures
(in rice equivalents)   80,000 kgs
_____

ΔY_1 = Net Increase in Expenditures$_1$ 120,000 kgs @1.50 pesos/kg = 180,000 pesos

Rice Proportion of Total Expenditure Now 25%

Increase in Rice Expenditures   40,000 kgs
Increase in other Expenditures
(in rice equivalents)   220,000 kgs

ΔY_2 = Net Increase in Expenditures$_2$ 260,000 kgs @1.50 pesos/kg = 390,000 pesos
ΔY_2 - Y_1 = 210,000 pesos = absolute consumer's surplus increase

Calculation of Absolute Consumer's Surplus, Engel's Law Assumptions

Before Road, Necessities = 3/4% of Total Expenditures
    Discretionary Income, Total Expenditures over Necessities   75, 000 pesos

After Road, Necessities = 2/3% of Total Expenditures
    Discretionary Income, Total Expenditures over Necessities   280, 000 pesos
    Increase in Discretionary Income = Consumer's Surplus   205, 000 pesos

the sequence in which investments ought to be undertaken nor the implications of that sequence for the achievement of any announced national goal.   Yet having uttered these caveats, we must insist that in any case, it is of vital importance to have used the more careful and accurate analysis to have obtained a measure of economic benefit regardless of the political context.

Notes to Appendix A

[1]Obviously a good deal has been written, and indeed well
written on this subject. Among the better sources are George
M. Smerk, Urban Transportation, the Federal Role (Blooming-
ton, Indiana: Indiana University Press, 1965); David M. Winch,
The Economics of Highway Planning (Toronto, Canada: University of Toronto Press, 1965); Hans A. Adler "Economic Evaluation Transport Projects, " in Gary Fromm, Transport Investment and Economic Development (Washington, D. C.: The
Brookings Institution, 1965); among others. See also, Clell
Harral, Preparation and Appraisal of Transport Projects (Washington, D. C.: The Brookings Institution, 1965). (Mimeographed.)

[2]See Leon V. Hirsch, "The Littoral Highway in El
Salvador, " in The Impact of Highway Investment on Development
(Washington, D. C.: The Brookings Institution, 1966).

[3]The Economic Commission for Latin America has made
frequent use of this general benefit concept. See, for example,
Economic Development of Colombia (Mexico City: ECLA, 1958).
In country planning the income elasticities of demand are used to
predict changes in demand levels as well as in the structure of
demand and of production.

[4]Harral, op. cit., pp. 52, 53.

[5]Barbara Bergmann, "The Cochabamba-Santa Cruz Highway
in Bolivia, " in The Impact of Highway Investment on Development,
loc. cit.

[6]Harral, op. cit., pp. 78, 79.

[7]See Arthur Wubnig and George B. Baldwin, "Measuring the
Benefits of Agricultural Feeder Road Projects, " Economic Development Institute of the International Bank for Reconstruction
and Development, a special lecture.

[8]Cf. John R. Hicks, A Revision of Demand Theory (Oxford,
England: Oxford University Press, 1956), pp. 186, 187.

[9]Cf. Alfred Marshall, Principles of Economics, 8th Edition,
footnote to page 125. Marshall felt his consumer's surplus could
be used as an index of economic development.

[10] For a discussion on various kinds of consumer surpluses, see my The Development and Use of the Consumer's Surplus, Ph. D. dissertation at Boston University, 1950, especially Chapter 3.

[11] Cf. Barbara Bergmann, Transportation in the Strategy of Bolivian Development (Washington, D. C.: The Brookings Institution, 1963), p. 40 (Mimeographed.)

APPENDIX B

TRANSPORT AND ECONOMIC DEVELOPMENT:
A PLANNING MODEL

In this appendix, we present a model which relates a proposed transport investment--a bridge, a highway, an airport, a pipe-line, a railway, a major harbor improvement, and the like-- to the resultant change in the pace of economic development. It is called a planning[1] model because it outlines the proposed action to be taken, indicates why it ought to be taken, spells out the problems in the undertaking, examines the probable changes in the environment to be served by the transport investment, all against the background of measures of likely achievement.

The basic elements of the model are the following:

Strategies: sets of available decisions and the time paths
                of actions resulting from those decisions.

Environments: the social, political, economic, geographical,
                as well as technological and knowledge elements
                of the societal complex to be affected by and
                likely to affect the transport investment.

Achievements: measures of the results, seen either beforehand
                or determined afterward, as indicators of the
                pace or changing stages of economic development.

The object of the model is to maximize achievements or minimize negative achievements by the selection of the "proper" strategy or strategies subject to the environment.

In analytical terms, a strategy S_i would be one of a definable set of n strategies ΣS_i (l = 1. 2........ n). An environment E_j would be an "effective" combination of environmental elements available from a set ΣE_j (j = 1. 2........ m). Whether there are more strategies or less than the number of possible environments is unknown though it is generally supposed that n $<$ m.

Achievements, Y_{ij} are indicators such that at least one measure of achievement is related to each of the possible combinations of strategies and environments.

199

The model operates as follows:

1. Only one strategy may be chosen at a time.

2. The environments are each distinct, though they may be related in some serial fashion.

3. The likelihood or probability, as well as the nature of each environment, is worked out in a forecast.

Thus, the object of the model is to select that S_i which will maximize (or minimize) Y_{ij} subject to some known probability for E_j. Each such maximand (or minimand) is a plan.

We can represent the strategies in various ways depending on the environment. If for example the environment is either completely known in advance or, what is more likely, tends to repeat itself with some known or determinable index of periodicity, then we may represent the strategy as a path through a network. That path will bear formal likeness to the "critical path" in network analysis. The events in the network are all environmental elements related to each other in some extensive fashion. [2]

To the extent that we know less and less about the probable periodicity of the network or what is worse, less and less about the component elements of the network and any possible environment which they may form, it becomes more and more difficult to represent the strategy.

If we know nothing or very little about possible environments, a statement which is equivalent to saying that we have very poor forecasting techniques, then the nature of the available strategies becomes very unclear. Under such conditions, at least two opposite temptations exist. One is to assume that any possible environment cannot differ greatly from what is already known and that as a consequence, the available strategies are familiar ones. The other is to assume that in the absence of adequate knowledge about possible environments, the probability of serious loss or ruin is quite high. Then the available strategies may reduce themselves to that set most likely to assist in avoiding ruin.

The above paragraph and the preceding one imply that though
strategies are independent of each other available strategy,
and though environments are distinct from each other, there
is a functional relationship between any one possible environment and an available strategy. This implication is correct
for the model, and probably for the real world. But that relationship is rather complex. In environmental networks with
known periodicities, there is usually one and only one critical
path. In that case, the strategies reduce themselves to poli-
cies--a known action sequence given the known or forecast
event relationship.

It is more likely, however, that the networks will be such that
more than one path and thus more than one strategy will be
critical in some sense. That sense is dependent upon the
emergent relationship among the events or elements of the
environmental network. That emergent relationship is subject
to forecast. Thus the strategy to be chosen may depend upon
the forecast rather more than upon the environmental network
itself.

In developing countries, especially those with severe geographical barriers, forecasts of the environment are very complex
indeed. Economic forecasting methods tend to be extrapolatory
in nature. [3] That is to say, they are based on models which take
the economic environment as given or which take the path of its
changes as given. The technique of forecasting, then, is to
pump into the model possible observations of the model variables
and grind out the forecast. What is needed are methods which
provide for structural changes in the economic models. This,
of course, is the contribution made by Schumpeter, Rostow,
Marx, Keynes, Kaldor, and other creators of the models of
"magnificent dynamics."[4]

However, have such models though obviously better than econo-
metrics or other forms of extrapolation sufficiently widened and
enlarged the set of possible environments? Have they taken
adequately into account the possible environmental networks that
could result from accidented geography, from different and less
"stable" political and social structures, from different timing
of the impact of new technologies, from different philosophical
orientations? All of these and more possible environmental
elements would seem to require a kind of forecasting that was
significantly broader in its coverage than that undertaken by

most economists. To be sure, the Lebret[5] School has made
some progress along these lines, though their work is little
known in Anglo-Saxon intellectual circles.

What this model does is to emphasize the role of forecasting.
While it is likely that rather more work needs to be done in increasing our knowledge about possible strategies, particularly
beyond that set derived largely from experience in advanced
countries, yet is is unlikely that much progress will be made
along this line unless better understanding is gained of the range
of possible environments in developing nations. The disadvan-
tage of much economic theory is not that it is wrong or inappli-
cable in developing nations, but rather that it implies a very
narrow range or set of environmental variables. This leads to
forecasting models and techniques which do not encompass
enough of the reality facing the decision-makers.

We need economic theories which will take account of the role
of organization, of social behavior within these organizations,
of the meaning and role of social objectives, of adaptability to
change, of information, and much more. Fortunately, in the
United States and Europe, we are at the threshhold of important
findings in all these areas. Planners in economic development
and especially in transport are hereby challenged to integrate
the emerging knowledge and techniques from management science
into their fields.

We have not exhausted the functional interrelationships in this
planning model, by any means. If it is to be asserted that strategies depend upon environments in many ways, it also is evident
that we could argue that environments themselves depend upon
achievements. In fact, each successive level of higher or lower
achievement might be taken to imply a different environment.
In a very simple fashion, Engel's Law has already been demonstrated to be a way of explaining what the demand and production
structures of an economy will be at each level of income. If we
know the range and pattern of income elasticities of demand,
we do have powerful prediction tools. An extension of this concept may suggest ways of working out the relationship between
achievement and environment.

By the same token, if we take potential levels of achievement
as the decision variables to be used in the selection among strategies, then we have a built-in relation which ties achievement

levels to strategies. Thus the "wrong" strategy might lead
not only to a lower than possible level of achievement, but
also to a different and presumably "worse" environmental
structure than could have been attained.

This model does not say which strategy ought to be undertaken.
Our knowledge about decision-making even under conditions of
considerable uncertainty has been improved significantly in
recent years. The benefits of that area of research are now
widely available for application. Some have mistakenly supposed
that models about decision-making were also planning models.
This has led to an over emphasis on search (e. g. , linear programming) and selection (e. g. , capital budgeting) techniques.
Linear programming in those kinds of planning models where
periodicity of environmental reformation is known and where
the selection of strategy is a matter of policy identifies the elements of a network though it cannot be used to generate the network itself. Capital budgeting shows us how to choose among
strategies (projects), but it assumes that the environment is
known, or at least that current forecasts of environment are
highly believable. This planning model takes advantage of what
we know to outline what more is necessary to be known to permit the attainment of the levels of achievement sought.

Notes to Appendix B

[1] For interesting and provocative comments on the nature of planning models, see: Martin K. Starr, "Planning Models," Management Science, December, 1966. See also, H. Igor Ansoff and Richard C. Brandenburg, "A Program of Research in Business Planning," Management Science, February, 1967; H. Igor Ansoff, Corporate Strategy (New York: McGraw-Hill, 1965).

[2] Extensive in the sense that each event is to be followed or preceded by at least one other.

[3] See C. J. Stokes, The Economics of Management (New York: Random House, 1968), Chapter 10.

[4] See W. J. Baumol, Economic Dynamics (New York: The Macmillan Company, 1951), Part I. Also C. J. Stokes, Crecimiento Economico (Santa Fe, Argentina: Prensa Universitaria del Litoral, 1964), Part I.

[5] Father L. J. Lebret is a Jesuit who has formed a school of economic development called "Economie et Humanisme" in Paris. For examples of his work and that of his school, see Suicide-Survie de l'Occident? (Paris: Les Editions Ouvrieres, 1953). Also, Michel Marie et al., Plan de Crecimiento del Distrito Valencia (Caracas: Editorial Arte, 1963).

ABOUT THE AUTHOR

Charles J. Stokes, Charles Anderson Dana Professor and Chairman of the Department of Economics at the University of Bridgeport, has been a student of Latin American economic development for many years. He has served as a Fulbright professor, visiting lecturer, State Department consultant and advisor, Ford Foundation consultant as well as industrial consultant at one time or other in most of the American nations since 1944. While on leave from the University of Bridgeport during the years 1963-65, he served as Director of Latin American Case Studies in Transportation at the Brookings Institution in Washington, D. C. and later both as Professor of Economic Development and Planning at the University of San Marcos in Lima, Peru, and as consultant to Tippets, Abbett, McCarthy, and Stratton. During this period much of the research that has led to this book was conducted.

Professor Stokes is the author of <u>Crecimiento Economico</u> (<u>Economic Growth</u>), a text on economic development for use in Latin American universities, published in Argentina in 1964. His articles have appeared in the principal economic journals of the Americas. He has been a delegate to a number of international conferences on Latin American economic problems and has served as an advisor to various Latin American governments.

Dr. Stokes studied economics at Boston University where he obtained his bachelor's, master's, and Ph. D. degrees. He also did postgraduate work at Columbia, Harvard, and Puerto Rico Universities and at the Massachusetts Institute of Technology.